Where Whippoorwills Sing

Also by Mary Cheek

A Forest Full of Flowers

Where Whippoorwills Sing

A Legacy of Love—A Family Heritage

Mary Elkins Cheek

iUniverse, Inc.

New York Lincoln Shanghai

Where Whippoorwills Sing
A Legacy of Love—A Family Heritage

iUniverse books may be ordered through booksellers or by contacting:

iUniverse
2021 Pine Lake Road, Suite 100
Lincoln, NE 68512
www.iuniverse.com
1-800-Authors (1-800-288-4677)

Because of the dynamic nature of the Internet, any Web addresses or links contained in this book may have changed since publication and may no longer be valid.

The views expressed in this work are solely those of the author and do not necessarily reflect the views of the publisher, and the publisher hereby disclaims any responsibility for them.

ISBN: 978-0-595-43839-6 (pbk)
ISBN: 978-0-595-68352-9 (cloth)
ISBN: 978-0-595-88164-2 (ebk)

Printed in the United States of America

Dedication

A special debt of gratitude to my parents, Tatum Thomas Elkins and Alma Joy Elkins, for the rich memories and their many sacrifices for our entire family. To my husband, Wayne, for his insights, suggestions, encouragement and support. To our four children and their spouses, Eric, Bonita and Rafael, John and Tina, Laurie and our four most wonderful precocious young grandchildren, John, Ava, Johnathon, and Katelyn. I hope they will someday read these recorded memories and know I left them and other descendents not yet born and future generations, a legacy and history of their roots and who they are.

Mary Elkins Cheek
February 23, 2006
Greensboro, North Carolina

Country Treasures

Sights and sounds of country life abound
Treasures of night and day all around.

The coo of mourning doves at dawn
A whippoorwill calling its' mate so strong.

A chorus of crickets' nightly song
soothes the soul
Fireflies aglow; like bits of stardust dancing
in the dark from heaven's gold.

Fallow soil is plowed and seeds
renew the sod
Working in perfect partnership with God.

Bees buzzing in clover fields of white
Seem to honor God in all their busy flight.

So beautiful the country flowers abound
Lifting heads toward heaven's crown.

Lowing of cattle in pastures green;
Lovely meadow flowers so serene.

A newborn calf on wobbly legs; brown
eyes bright
'Tis a miracle of life with sheer delight.

Windswept waves of golden grain;
bowing heads in prayer
Heavens hand of boundless beauty
so joyfully declare.

Fresh country air, so clean and clear
like sparkling morning dew;
We breathe God's love and care
each day anew.

He who sees sunset's breathless beauty
and bids his soul be still;
Will surely feel God's presence there
and know that He is real.

Mary Elkins Cheek

Where Whippoorwills Sing

Lovely country twilights magic afterglow
Sunsets golden picture show
Paint flowing reflections
In still waters far below.

Blue dragonflies skim the peaceful pond,
Rest on cattails soft til early dawn,
Bullfrogs splash rippling waters, bravely sing
Floating free top dewdrop lily pad perfection.

Fireflies like flickering starlight take flight
Signal silently with wondrous delight
Mingle country meadows, yonder treetops tall
Span natures sparkling songs of light.

Distant whippoorwills sing keenly clear
Ever longing for its mate ... elusive, seldom seen
Each soulful song brings God's peaceful presence
Heavens nighttime gift so near.

Melodious mysteries of summer sounds
Only found in sheer forest shadows
Where country whippoorwills sing
There life's true beauty abounds.

Mary Elkins Cheek
Harriet H. Barrett

Content

Acknowledgements xv

Preface xvii

Introduction xix

Part I—Farm Memories 1

Spring Planting and Buried Treasure 3

Gardening, Gathering, and Preserving 5

Gathering the Golden Grains 9

Corn Shucking Time 10

Wood—The Warmth of Winter 12

Fatted Pigs and Winter Feasts 14

A Long Winter's Night 17

Farm Hunting for All Seasons 19

Christmastime in the Country and Mistletoe over the Door 20

The Rock and the Last Laugh 23

School Memories 24

Old MacDonald's Farm and the Pony Tale 27

Healthy Choices and Chicken Soup 30

Summer Fun and City Cousins 32

Summer Storms and Old Time Remedies 36

The Gathering Spot 38

Scary Times 40

Mystery Plants and Hidden Secrets 42

Rich City Mice and Poor Country Cousins 43

Health History 45

Sleep Walkers: Asleep and Awake 46

Balancing Love, Work, Play and Discipline. 47

Horse Sense. 50

Snapshots of Farm Memories 51

    Raising the Roof. *51*

    Strong Nails—A Child's Remedy. *51*

    Gone Fishing. *51*

    A Quarter Bribe. *52*

    The Traveling Salesman *52*

    Swing High, Swing Low. *52*

    Brave Little Lad. *53*

    Another Narrow Escape *53*

    A Free Fish Tale. *53*

    Little Green Apples. *54*

    Not M & M's. *54*

Treasures from Home 56

Part II—Parents and Beloved Lulee **59**

My Parents—Alma Joy Elkins and Tatum Thomas Elkins. 62

Mama Knew Best 65

Mama's Lovely Legacy of Flowers 70

Mama's Family—The Lamberts. 74

Daddy—Ruler of the Roost 75

Our Beloved Lulee 82

Part III—Descendents **89**

Family Descendents—From England to the Civil War 92

Children Grow Up But the Farm Never Leaves Them 97

Part IV—A Legacy of Flowers. 103
Mama's Legacy Continues In My Own Garden 105

Appendix. 109
Freedom and Liberty for All 111
America—Preference or Principle 112

Afterword 117

About the Author 119

Acknowledgements

I owe a special debt of gratitude to my daughter, Bonita, for inspiring me to pen experiences and rich memories of growing up on our family farm; also, for assistance in editing, arranging and typing my original drafts. Thanks to my six siblings for their contribution of memories and pictures. I am truly grateful and thankful to all.

I gratefully acknowledge the immense effort from my brother, retired Lt. Colonel Jim T. Elkins, of Stafford, Virginia for his long hours and months of research in the archives and libraries and talking with many descendants compiling the historical accounts of our family's heritage. This was an enormous undertaking and I could not have had this information without his unselfish contribution to this section of my book.

Also, to my niece, Julia Vadersen, for guiding and editing my book to completion with her knowledge and expertise learned during her years as library media specialist and administrator for Virginia Beach City Public Schools, Virginia Beach, Virginia. I am so grateful for her labor of love.

Preface

My goal in writing this memoir is to take my readers back in time and paint pictures of real experiences of farm life and glimpses of other times and places.

Happy and carefree sunny summers and cold snowy winters are balanced with experiencing healthy country living. My book is a collection of short stories and reflections from my life on the family farm with childhood experiences that shaped who I am today and what I believe.

As I penned these reflections, I found that growing up on a farm in the country had numerous benefits for me. Here, I developed a love of nature and respect for our natural resources. I gained spiritual insight while experiencing the wonders of our amazing world, knowing that God reveals Himself if we take the time to look. Being raised in a large family taught me much discipline, a measure of unselfishness, and the necessity to consider others. Respect for all regardless of race was a valuable lesson learned from our beloved Lulee. Natural foods, fresh air, and pure water made me realize the many health benefits and the importance of conservation of our natural resources.

Farm life helped me build personal character traits including sharing, kindness, self-sufficiency, and reverence for life and all God's creatures. I realized the importance of love for family and to appreciate all our freedoms and sacrifices my ancestors made.

If I give back a measure of the enjoyment I've received writing and sharing these memories, I will indeed be richly rewarded.

Introduction

Recording our memories is like going back in a time warp; a happy and sad feeling remembering each detail as though it were happening again, and somehow longing to experience it yet again if only in our mind, soul, and heart. Reflecting back on time puts you into another place even just for a little while. We see, feel, and experience a time gone by as we put these poignant memories into words. Reflections of life capture the essence of who we really are today. We want time to stand still for a moment as we savor these memories. It heals, grounds, and makes us whole and able to experience today in more meaningful ways. I think what matters most and always will is character and spiritual insight. Money, fame, or a thousand educational degrees cannot teach you these values. In the final analysis, we are all alike: searching, spinning on our little blue planet Earth and looking for the meaning in and of our lives.

By today's standards some might consider growing up on a farm a hard life, but as I reflect back, fresh air, clean water, having animals near and nature all around teaches about life itself. Living close to the land and observing nature has so much to offer. It builds discipline and character as well as many other values. Most importantly, it confirms God's love and care for us in so many ways. The beautiful evening sunsets over the pond, the distant song of the whip-

Mary at twelve years old in the seventh grade.

poorwill at dusk and countless other confirmations of God's creative work in our world were there for all to experience. Especially the beautiful flowers on our farm I loved so much! I like to think God smiled and there were flowers! Two favorite old Chinese proverbs express my feelings: "If you would be happy all your life, plant a garden!" and "Happiness is holding two white hyacinths in both hands."

We were blessed to experience all of these things. To share them with others is indeed a privilege. Come along with me as I reflect back on a life that helped me find a deeper meaning and wholeness for my posterity. My answers are rooted in my childhood experiences on our family farm. You may find yours in other ways, but it will begin with those early years of life's experiences.

I grew up in Chatham County, North Carolina, located in the Central Piedmont area, in the nineteen thirties and forties on a large 150 acre farm

with three brothers and three sisters. I hope these reflections will be a rich legacy for our children, their children, and other family members as well as a glimpse of farm life in another time for others. Since our working family farms are fast disappearing and becoming a thing of the past, these vignettes demonstrate life on the farm from one person's perspective. Recording our personal memoirs links one generation to another and is so valuable in search of our roots and family history. It helped me to learn who I am and what shaped my life.

We had a working farm with several support buildings in addition to the main farmhouse. The barn to house the horses, mules, and cows was made of large hand-hewn logs with pegs. It had an upstairs loft where hay was stored. Straw was stored in a log house made of hand-hewn logs and pegs. Riding atop the horse-drawn wagon piled high with hay for the barn is a fond memory. I can still smell the freshly mown hay....

There was a two-story granary with large bins to store the wheat and oats, horses' bridles, the apple cider press and many other farm items. Gallons of apple cider vinegar were made, then poured into large glass and earthenware jugs for storage in the granary.

The smokehouse was dark red and used for curing and storing hams, shoulders, stuffed sausage and other pork meats. The meat was covered with salt for about two weeks and hung to cure, then smoked a couple of days with hickory bark. A generous amount of black pepper was applied to protect the meat from insects or rodents that might get into the tightly sealed smokehouse. The corn crib was essential for storing the many bushels of corn needed to feed the livestock. It was constructed with slats and crib wire on the sides and back for air circulation and to keep the troublesome weevils out as well as rodents.

Another important building was the blacksmith shop. Horseshoes were made here and the horses were shod. Farm machinery pieces were made and repaired here as well. I remember a coal forge with a blower for heating metal and a large anvil for shaping the hot metal. I was fascinated watching the sparks fly as the anvil and large hammer shaped the steel. My father knew much about working in the blacksmith shop since he had worked in his father's shop in Siler City. His father, my grandfather, at one time owned a drugstore and several rental properties as well.

Other buildings on our farm included a generator house for electricity and a pump enclosure for running water and a well house. There were wood houses with sheds, one for logs for the fireplaces and another for the stoves. There were pig pens, a chicken house and five sheds for machinery and farm equipment storage and several large pastures.

As children, we enjoyed carefree summers picking colorful wildflowers and watching the horses and cows grazing lazily. These are all poignant memories. I can still hear the soft lowing of the cows as they switched their tails in the warm summer sun. In the late afternoon, they lay down, usually under a shade tree, and quietly chewed their cud, seeming to be at perfect peace. One call at feeding time and they raced to the barn to be fed their nightly meal of bran. The cows were also milked at this time. They rewarded us with gallons of fresh, rich milk free from hormones and antibiotics so prevalent in our milk today. Home-churned butter and buttermilk were other delicious rewards. The birth of baby calves was also an exciting time on the farm. Our cows, horses and other animals were an important part of farm life.

There were fields for growing wheat, corn and other grains for the livestock and our own use. Often, lighted lanterns were carried to the barn after dark to tend and feed the livestock. I still have and treasure one of the old lanterns that was used. The process of planting and sowing crops began in early spring and continued until late fall. The picking and harvesting of those crops began the rewards and the fruits of our labors. Looking back, one can reflect with greater objectivity on events and remembrances that highlight and describe a way of life as it really was lived.

So begins the account of my growing up years on the family farm.

A delightful poem written by my youngest daughter, Laurie, is reminiscent of the meadows of home.

Springtime Meadows

I'm planted in meadows underground
There are more of me for miles around.

I'm growing so fast
Living in soil is a thing of the past.

Very soon I'll hit the top
I'll breathe the air and then I'll stop.

Mary Elkins Cheek.

I'll sprout my leaves and drink the rain
I'm growing and growing with colors to gain.

My petals are the beetles' bed
Then I look up into a honeybee's head.

I'm surrounded by God's love and powers
Yes! I'm a thousand springtime flowers.

Laurie Cheek

PART I

Farm Memories

Spring Planting and Buried Treasure

The farm was a model of self-sufficiency. Everything was grown, stored, or canned to be used throughout the cold winter months until spring came when the process began again and lasted into late fall.

Growing up near nature and observing the beautiful world reminds you that each day is a gift. Everything on earth has its own time and its own reason, season, and purpose. How important it is to fulfill our purpose as well. Planting time and harvest time reminds me of the little verse: "He who plants a seed beneath the sod and waits to see, believes in God."

Springtime began with plowing and planting the corn and other field and garden crops. After Daddy went into law enforcement in 1932, he began hiring live-in farm workers. This continued for about eight years. We had five different workers who were paid five to eight dollars per month, plus room and board. This placed an additional burden on our mother as she always had to prepare three large meals each day. Farm workers were always hungry!

It was not easy for my brothers as they carried on full-time farming while attending eight-month school terms. However, they were able to do it, even increasing crop acreage and production. It involved working before and after school hours as well as on Saturdays, holidays and the summer out-of-school months. The term "school vacation time" was indeed a misnomer to say the least. There were lots of planning and instruction from our father as well as long hours of work on the farm.

Those golden grains were not the only buried treasure. My brothers found arrowheads buried long ago in the freshly plowed rows of corn. More arrowheads were unearthed in the bottom land near the creek. Native Americans are thought to have lived in the Chatham County area centuries before the settlers arrived. Tribes specific to the region included the Cape

Fear Indians: the Eno, the Sissapahaw, and the Keyawees. They left these artifacts on the land so many moons ago as they lived and hunted for food. The Indians depended on the land for everything and greatly respected it as Mother Earth, a lesson for us to learn today. All too often the land is polluted as we destroy our natural, valuable resources. We are just stewards of what is given and then it's passed on to other generations. We need to be good stewards of our most precious gifts of land, water, and air or else we could completely desecrate the land and make it a concrete jungle with few trees, poison our water and pollute the very air we breathe. Not much of a legacy there....

My daughter, Laurie, shares a poem she wrote to remind us how our forests and natural areas are being destroyed.

Where Is My Tree?

I'm a baby bird; I live in a nest
I chirp for my mother; I know I'm a pest.

I stretch for my food; I hear a sound
The next thing I know
I'm upon the ground.

They cut down my tree!
Is this how my world is going to be?

Why are the animals fleeing so fast?
Is our wonderful forest
a thing of the past?

Where is my tree?
Apartment complexes are all I can see
They put up a birdfeeder instead for me.

Laurie Cheek

Gardening, Gathering, and Preserving

Gardening, canning and preserving the fruits of our labors (and what labor it was!) made the farm almost self-sufficient. A great variety of food was produced including meat, milk, butter and breads made from our own milled wheat and corn.

There was a cider mill for making apple cider from our orchard apples. Apple cider was stored and fermented, turning into vinegar. This would give us an entire year's supply of vinegar.

Before the apple cider turns to vinegar, there is an in-between stage of cider called "hard cider". That is a story in itself. It could give you a "buzz" in a hurry! Mama would not allow us to drink hard cider—she thought it would make you drunk!

My oldest brother, Jim, made locust beer from the fruit of the locust tree growing in our pasture. This fruit has a jelly-like consistency inside long black pods hanging from the tree. They were picked and put in a barrel with sugar and water added. After some time, the brew was drained off with a spigot at the bottom. It tasted much like apple cider.

Gardening began in early spring and continued until late fall. Early crops included spring onions, garden peas, lettuce, radishes, and all cool season crops. Later, tomatoes, cucumbers, okra, cabbage, potatoes, squash, green peppers, and corn were planted. Watermelons and cantaloupes were grown by the wagon-load.

Later in the season the fun began. Potatoes were harvested (oh, my aching back just thinking of picking up all those tubers!) and sprinkled with lime to prevent them from spoiling. We stored potatoes in the granary, barn, and under our house crawl space for use in the winter. I didn't like the dirty job of harvesting those potatoes but was rewarded with and enjoyed delicious potato salad and many other dishes. This taught us to appreciate hard work and values like sowing and reaping. As children we often wondered why we needed to reap so much!

In the fall, sweet potatoes were dug and stored. We grew them by the wagon-load. The vines were saved and fed to the pigs and cows. Nothing on a farm is wasted.

There was a large persimmon tree in the pasture. Everyone enjoyed the fruit when it fell. Even the possums enjoyed them for persimmons are their favorite food. We enjoyed persimmon pudding which is a Southern dessert made from very ripe persimmons. It is essential that they are gathered on the ground when they have fallen and are fully ripe. Otherwise, they will be bitter.

Persimmon Pudding

2 cups persimmon pulp
3 eggs
2 cups sugar
2 cups all-purpose flour
1 tsp. baking soda

½ cup butter, melted
1 tsp. vanilla extract
1 cup buttermilk
1 small grated raw sweet potato

Beat eggs and dry ingredients. Add melted butter and vanilla and mix well. Add milk, grated sweet potato and stir. Add the persimmon pulp last and blend into mixture. Pour into a greased 9 x 13 pan. Bake 350 for 45 to 50 minutes. Top with whipped cream or vanilla ice cream.

Pumpkins were gathered from the corn field. We grew herbs, especially sage, to be incorporated into sausage along with hot peppers. We harvested vegetables and canned hundreds of jars for winter use.

Several methods were used to keep food cold in those good old days before electricity was available. First, there was an icebox to keep food from spoiling. The ice man came once or twice weekly to put two large blocks of ice into the upper portion of the icebox. He brought it in with huge ice tongs. The bottom part stayed cold and worked very well. As children, we looked forward to the ice man coming as he gave us chips of ice from his truck to enjoy and help stay cool in the summertime. Mama chipped large chunks of ice with an ice pick to make lemonade, our favorite summertime refreshment. Later, there was a large refrigerator with two kerosene burners at the bottom that you had to light. After electricity became available, we used electrical powered ones.

Food was also kept with some help from Mother Nature. Lulee and John Watson, who lived on our farm, had a rock covered spring with steps leading down to the cool water which helped keep food cold. A lard bucket with a tight lid and attached string was used to submerge milk, butter and food into the cool spring water. There it stayed until it was needed.

Our supply of blackstrap molasses came from a neighbor who grew sugar cane each year. The cane stalks were put between rollers to extract the sap. This was put into a huge vat, slowly stirred until it became thick and just the right consistency for making blackstrap molasses.

Maple syrup is made in a similar way. My brother Ted, who lives in Minnesota, explained to me how maple syrup is tapped and cooked in much the same way as the sugar cane. Many hours of cooking produces pure maple syrup. It takes thirty two gallons of sap to make one gallon of syrup. This, like molasses, is really a labor of love. We wonder why it is so expensive.

All kinds of fruits were picked, canned, and preserved for jellies and jams. Oh how good the preserves were with those hot biscuits and home churned butter! We were living high on the hog and didn't know it! Trucks came by selling peaches for one dollar per bushel and on that day several bushels were canned. Peanuts were grown, dried in the sun and stored. Summertime fun was wild strawberry and blackberry hunting. More was eaten than saved and we brought home more "chiggers" than berries! Chiggers are tiny red bugs that make you itch! It was a little adventure to see who could find the largest wild strawberry patch and race to it first. Occasionally, we encountered a black snake in the berry patches.

This reminds me of a neighbor who barely escaped stepping on a black snake in her strawberry patch. The snake began to chase her and as she ran her large straw hat fell off. After all the excitement she returned to retrieve the hat, and much to her dismay, the snake had coiled itself under that hat and the chase was on again! A true story as unlikely as it sounds. Black snakes are not poisonous but will bite if provoked. They are friendly to the environment since they eat mice and other rodents that destroy crops.

Needless to say, we grew most of our food. A few staples were purchased including coffee and tea. It is not good that today more is wasted than consumed. Remember, waste not, want not.

Gathering the Golden Grains

Spring and fall harvesting was a busy time. After threshing the golden wheat in the field, it went into granary bins for storage. It would be later bagged and taken to the grist mill for grinding. A large wagon pulled by a team of horses was used to transport the wheat and corn which was milled into flour and corn meal. The wagon and horses were central to the farm until a tractor gradually replaced them.

The freshly milled flour was used to make biscuits. Still hot from the oven, butter and preserves were added to the biscuits. A variety of preserves such as fig, plum, strawberry, blackberry, peach, pear, grape and cherry preserves were available to serve up on those buttery biscuits. One special fruit we enjoyed were damson preserves as we had several trees. This dark, purple fruit made delicious preserves. Asiatic plums originated from Damascus. One can only guess when and how these trees came to this country. Often neighbors came to gather damsons when they ripened.

We also enjoyed biscuits and country ham with red-eye gravy. Red-eye gravy is made from the juices of country cooked ham. Also our fresh eggs and sausage are mouth watering memories of breakfast.

Our family shared so much of what we had with others, and they with us. A lovely custom for us to follow today. Give and it shall be given is so true as we receive much more when we share.

Gathering the corn from the fields was a labor-intensive process. The corn was picked by hand in the fall along with the gathering of pumpkins planted in the corn rows. We had our pick of pumpkins for carving into funny faces for Halloween and pumpkin pies. I remember those pies with the distinctive aroma of cinnamon and other spices.

Corn Shucking Time

Dried corn from the fields was picked in the early fall and brought into the farmyard and put into one long pile. All the neighborhood men and boys came together and took turns at each farm helping shuck the corn. The women helped each other prepare the evening meal. Everyone sat in chairs along the long row of corn. As they shucked the corn, they threw it over the un-shucked pile and made another pile of shucked corn. They threw the shuck behind them and kept going until the corn was finished.

The corn was stored in the corn crib to feed the animals year round. The shucks were stored to feed the livestock. Corn shucking time was a social event where neighbors helped each other and shared stories. After many hours of shucking, all enjoyed a late evening feast. This built a strong sense of community. Mama's cooking was praised—cakes, pies, old-fashioned sweet potato pudding, fried chicken and much more.

Mama's Old Fashioned Grated Sweet Potato Pudding
My Favorite Recipe

4 cups grated raw sweet potatoes
½ cup sugar
½ cup corn syrup
1 ½ cups milk
1/3 cup butter
3 eggs
1 tsp. nutmeg
1 tsp. cinnamon
½ tsp. salt

Mary Elkins Cheek.

Peel the sweet potatoes. Add the sugar and corn syrup to the milk. Grate the sweet potatoes into the sweetened milk to prevent discoloring. Add beaten eggs. Melt the butter and add to the mixture along with other ingredients. Pour into a buttered baking pan and cook at 350 degrees for about an hour, stirring every 15 minutes. Let crust form and do not stir last 15 minutes (coconut, raisins and nuts may be added). Yummy when served with a dollop of whipped cream.

Wood—The Warmth of Winter

Anticipating the long, cold winter months, a priority was to have all the wood houses packed full by fall. Trees were cut down and sawed into logs and hauled by wagon into the wood sawing area. Long logs were sawed into shorter logs for the fireplaces and stoves. Slabs which are trimmed pieces from the logs were obtained from sawmill sites and used for kitchen stove wood.

An axe was used to split the wood for the fireplace. Some wood was left large to have as back logs. The logs were stacked with smaller logs placed in front of larger ones. Pungent pine kindling wood went under smaller logs to quickly start the fires. Each night hot coals were covered up with the ashes to help start our morning fires.

I remember popping many batches of popcorn using a wire basket with a long handle over those wood fires. It was held over the fire in the fireplace and shaken until the corn popped. We poured a generous amount of home-churned butter and salt over it. Delicious!

Our kitchen stove needed wood throughout the year and a large fireplace burning wood about fifteen hours a day during heating season; large volumes of wood were consumed and required great amounts of labor. It took lots of time and energy to get the wood ready for winter use.

A near tragedy occurred while gathering wood with our team of horses and wagon. Brothers, Jim and Ted, were bringing a load of wood back to the farm. As they were going down an incline and putting on brakes, Ted lost his balance and fell between the wagon wheels. Jim was driving and, as he looked back, clearly saw the wheel run over Ted's head. Evidently, a rock prevented the full impact of the wheel across his head.

Jim stopped the team of horses, ran back and put Ted into the wagon and raced home. Ted was a bloody mess, but alive and not as seriously injured as expected. He carries a large scar to this day from the impact of the wheel. I know a miracle angel intervened and watched over Ted on that day for sure.

Fatted Pigs and Winter Feasts

When the weather became cold in late fall, it was hog killing time. Before hogs were killed, they were confined in a pen and fed more often. This fattened them up, increasing weight before slaughtering them. The hog was killed with a pistol and allowed to bleed out by cutting its throat. The girls were never allowed to witness this, but we heard the shots. The hog was then pulled on a sled by a horse and taken to an outside fireplace where it was dipped into a huge rectangular vat of boiling water with wood ashes added. This process helped release hair from the hog so it could be scraped off. At that point, the pig was split open with entrails removed and placed in a large tin tub which would be made later into chitterlings.

Nothing from the hog was wasted. Hams, shoulders and sides of bacon were salted down and hung in the smokehouse to cure. Sausage was made by grinding meat through a sausage mill, adding salt, red pepper and sage. Sausage making and the like was usually done by Mama with all the girls learning and assisting her.

Pork tenderloins were cut along with spareribs and backbones. Souse or pickled meat was made from the head and other parts. The feet were boiled after removing hooves by putting them in hot coals. They were then pickled or dipped into a batter and fried. The liver was cooked and made into an onion spiced pudding as well as frying it when fresh. Fat from the hog was rendered in a huge black pot. This lard was used for frying and cooking.

The leftover fried-out meat became what is called "cracklings". The crackling cornbread with turnip greens and black-eye peas was real country soul food. Striped fat back was for breakfast bacon and flavoring vegetables. Even the entrails were emptied, washed many times and boiled in the big black pot. These became the chitterlings. They smelled so bad they had to be prepared in the wash house pot. Some of the raw entrails were used for stuffing certain sausages. This sausage was hung to dry and cure in the smokehouse.

Lye soap was made from leftover fat combined with fireplace ashes. This homemade soap was used for washing clothes. It tended to give the user dishpan hands in a hurry!

For our large family, we usually butchered five or six hogs each winter. They generally weighed four hundred pounds each, amounting to about two thousand four hundred pounds of pork utilized per year. The butchering process was phased with two hogs at a time in intervals of four to six weeks. This phasing allowed consumption of fresh products with a minimum of preserving procedures. The work that was required is hard to imagine. All who helped with butchering the hogs received a lunch of fresh tenderloins, fried liver with onions and lots of gravy and biscuits.

Pork contains a lot of saturated fat, but we had a more active, hardworking lifestyle back then. It didn't contain harmful nitrates and nitrites prevalent in meat today.

Butchering the hogs took place before dawn. One particular time, my brothers Jack and Ted were sent across to the neighbor's house to ask Mr. Moore for some help. In the meantime, Jim hid in some bushes along the road to play a practical joke on his brothers. When Ted and Jack came back by, they heard strange noises and hit the ground running back home scared half to death! They both still remember that scare so well. Wonder what they thought was in the bushes?

There were pig tales to tell. My brother, Jim, told the hilarious tale of hog killing time gone awry. Since our father was a sheriff, he was an expert with his pistol or so we thought. Dad prided himself on the fact that he never needed but one bullet to kill a hog. The hog had to be shot in just the precise place. This particular time he missed. The hog began running around the pen with four other hogs all squealing loudly as Dad gave chase to get the final shot. This spooked the horse which was hitched to a sled, waiting just outside the pen. The horse bolted, running as fast as he could; the sled bouncing behind him. Meanwhile, Dad was frantically chasing the hog. He kept shooting, missing, and running in circles while the hogs kept squealing and running around the pen. Finally, in desperation, he was forced to cut the hog's throat to put him down. As they butchered the hog, stray bullets were found in all the wrong places. That ended Dad's claim to fame of expert marksmanship at least in the hog killing arena.

Butchering animals may seem to some as cruel and unnecessary. But this was an important source of food supply for the long cold winter months.

A Long Winter's Night
Hand-made Quilts and Down Feather Mattresses

Wintertime was usually snowy and always cold, but all stayed warm even though there was no central heat. At night we snuggled in down feather mattresses with blankets and hand-made quilts. Occasionally, when we awoke, we found ice in the glass on the nightstand; however, we always kept warm. Children today would be mortified to sleep in an unheated bedroom and/or no air conditioning in the summer! Me too! I've grown accustomed to our modern conveniences.

My older brother, Jim, would warm the house by rising early in the morning to start fires in the fireplace and kitchen stove. In later years, my mother did this. Before we got up, the house was warm and Mama was cooking breakfast—I can smell that country ham frying!

Before we had electricity, oil lamps were used for lighting. I remember an Aladdin lamp that had a very bright glowing mantle which was a big improvement over regular oil lamps. This was the latest thing in lighting, or so we thought!

Even though we didn't have electricity like today, our lights never went out as they may do today because there was a gas generator to provide electricity. Additionally we did have our privately owned but shared telephone line so we were not completely primitive! There was a "party line" arrangement with about five neighbors, each having a distinct ring.

During World War II, public electricity arrived. Running water was generated in the pump house from our well but indoor plumbing was limited due to a poor supply of well water. Our water resources were scarce, especially during hot, dry summers as we had only well water. Many wells went dry during this time. I don't remember our well going dry but do recall my brothers frequently hauling water from the nearby spring, which was always abundant, for the livestock and clothes washing. To haul the water, a large oak barrel was set on a sled and filled with water from the spring, located about one fourth mile away. A horse pulled the sled with water to the house. In another barrel, rain water was collected as it ran from the tin roof. This barrel was waxed on the inside to make it completely waterproof. These huge barrels were originally used for making "moonshine" liquor at stills. I'm sure this barrel came from a "moonshine" raid as it smelled like fermented mash. This water was used only for washing clothes and sometimes for watering our flowers.

Eventually larger watering ponds were dug in the pasture to provide adequate water for our livestock. We experienced a water problem due to only a fifty foot well which was inadequate to supply all the water that was really needed. Running into extremely hard blue flint rock required extensive blasting with dynamite. We finally gave up on having a deeper well.

Even today, there are water shortages with our cities' water supply and all are forced to conserve. Everyone is encouraged to use rain barrels once again so I guess we are still at the mercy of God and Mother Nature as we always have been. Only now we tend to think we are self sufficient and don't need God anymore, but in reality one can do nothing without the mercy of God. Indeed, the very air we breathe is but one example of how dependent one is on His grace. He owns it all. The cattle on a thousand hills! All are just temporary stewards of what we have. That should humble us a bit! Country life tends to make you more aware and appreciate our God-given natural resources.

Farm Hunting for All Seasons

My brothers Jim, Jack, and Ted always placed rabbit boxes along the pasture fences and checked them often. Especially when it snowed, the rabbits went into the boxes for shelter and were trapped. They brought them home and Mama made rabbit stew or fried rabbit. Delicious with hot biscuits and gravy! This was a great supplement to our usual pork.

In spring and summer, the boys also went frog gigging, which is a way to catch frogs. Shining lights along the creek banks, they gigged frogs and saved the legs for frying. Often, the boys encountered as many snakes as frogs. If you have never eaten frog's legs, they taste much like chicken and are considered a delicacy today in many fine restaurants.

My brothers frequently hunted, usually bagging additional rabbits and other wildlife which were used for food. Friends from town liked to come to our farm to hunt. They especially liked to hunt quail. This bird is a gourmet item on menus today. My brothers knew where wild game could be found and how to have a successful hunt. Hunting dogs were kept to assist the hunters find their game.

Christmastime in the Country and Mistletoe over the Door

Christmastime was very special. After finding just the right cedar tree in the fields and cutting it down, our creative talents were used to decorate. Strings of popcorn, paper chains, sycamore balls covered with silver paper or dipped in silver paint, lots of icicles and glass balls adorned our tree. The tree had large brightly colored hot lights that were beautiful but dangerous. Why we didn't burn the house down I don't know! Probably because our tree was cut fresh from the hedgerow. Holly, boxwood, running cedar and assorted greenery decorated our home everywhere.

The night before Christmas was always exciting. As young children, we set out our own special chairs for Santa. It was a new doll for my sister and me and appropriate gifts for the rest of my siblings. Nuts, fruits and candies abounded since Daddy always bought a bushel of apples, oranges, tangerines and nuts.

We made fudge, mints, pulled candy, and Mama made a special Christmas cake. She did not have an exact recipe but seemed to know instinctively how to cook without exact measurements. She would bake a yellow two or three-layer cake, split the layers and fill them with fresh coconut, raisins, and nuts ground through the sausage mill. Caramel icing topped with pecan halves covered that yellow cake. It was then put in the glass-front china closet in the dining room.

We would sneak in there and pick the pecans halves off the top. When Mama discovered the nuts were missing from her beautiful labor of love creation for Christmas, she went on a "who did it" mission. Like a detective, she interrogated everyone until the culprit was found. When no one admitted being guilty, she lined everyone up and threatened to switch the whole lot of us unless someone confessed. That usually did the trick!

You might want to try Mama's Wonderful Christmas Cake.

For the cake: Make a two or three layer yellow cake. Bake as directed. Fill the layers of the cake with the coconut, raisin and nut filling. Ice the cake with Easy Caramel Icing.

Easy Caramel Icing Recipe

1 stick butter, (1/2 cup)
¾ cup light brown sugar
¾ cup dark brown sugar
¼ cup whole milk
2 cups powdered sugar
1 tsp. vanilla

Filling between the layers: grind coconut, raisins, and nuts together. You can add a little icing to hold the layers together.

Cook butter and sugar together until boiling. Add milk and bring back to a boil. Beat powdered sugar and vanilla into mixture until smooth. Add coconut, raisin, and nut mixture between layers and caramel mixture on top and sides of cake. Press pecan halves on top. Oh! So good!

My Aunt Luta made a table Christmas tree using thorn branches and stuck red, green and white frosty gum drops all over it. While visiting, I remember eating those gum drops off that tree. Just too much temptation! Aunt Luta

Sisters Florence, Margaret, and Mary frolic in the snow!

21

was a warm, generous person who would have given me the whole tree if I had asked.

Christmas snows were exciting and fun, too. We always made snow cream from the fallen snow. All enjoyed making snow cream each winter using milk, sugar, vanilla flavoring and sometimes cinnamon. It was a favorite wintertime dessert and so good!

When I was thirteen years old, one snowy winter night, the kids from town came down with sleds to play in the snow. All came in the house to warm up. One of the boys saw mistletoe over the door, leaned over, and kissed me! At thirteen, my first kiss under the mistletoe! I was in mild shock for a moment after that! He quickly shook me back to reality! A more innocent and gentler time. What a sweet memory....

Christmas should be a time of celebrating God's ultimate expression of love for mankind through Christ's birth, death and resurrection. Often children want everything they see and never get enough. It is important to remember, as in simpler times, that real Christmas means sharing our blessings with others less fortunate.

The Rock and the Last Laugh

Quietness was very precious growing up in a family of seven children. In our pasture was a huge rock which was a great place to go and sit to be alone and sort things out or just to dream. It was a great place to spend some quiet time. I went often to that rock and still need "the rock" for guidance and spiritual renewal for myself. In this fast-paced world, it is important to take time for quietness to acknowledge and find strength in a higher power. As I reflect back on these special times sitting on the rock, not realizing it at the time that I was getting in touch with my inner, spiritual, creative self.

While I was growing up, I remember thinking I was an ugly duckling (probably during my quiet time on the "rock"). My two younger brothers teased me about having naturally full lips. When I was about ten or twelve years old, suddenly I was hearing more complimentary remarks. Anyway, guess who got the last laugh! I was voted the cutest girl in my graduation class! So the joke was on my insensitive brothers! Aren't I lucky to have lips with such a full natural appearance which many people pay plastic surgeons thousands of dollars to get. So ironic!

School Memories

All children have been the target of teasing and bullying at one time or another. I remember my first day of school so long ago. I didn't enjoy that first day one bit! A little boy started chasing me and I fell and skinned my knee. My older sister, Frances, marched the little boy and me to the principal's office to show what he had done. The boy was so scared he couldn't speak. (I won't name names, but I still remember). He never tried that again! I had a big sister (thanks, Frances!) to defend me, but so many children aren't as lucky as I was. Teachers, parents, and others consistently work to eliminate bullying in our schools today. It is important to remember that every human being has infinite value because we were all created in God's image. Everyone deserves to be treated with dignity, respect and kindness. We all have special talents and a purpose for our life.

Seared into my memory are two special young people in our school. One had braces on her legs from polio and the other had a face deformity and was generally ignored by almost everyone. I remember feeling compassion and deliberately going up to them and talking. I most remember the appreciation I saw on their faces. How good I felt in my heart for recognizing them as people with feelings too! This taught me the importance of kindness.

I think we are much more compassionate and accept others with disabilities and handicaps today. There have been many positive changes and much less discrimination. Even mental illness is openly discussed and much work is being done to help those with mental illness today. There was a time when these things were "swept under the rug" and not openly discussed or acknowledged. I must say that is one thing that was not better in the "good ole days".

A fun memory of school days was attending a formal ball at Oak Ridge Military Academy with my high school sweetheart who was a cadet there. I wore a long, green gown with a velvet bodice and a sequined net wrap to match. The boys were dressed in formal military uniforms. We went under crossed swords entering the ballroom. What a magical evening to remember! I saved the dress and net wrap for many years. When my own children were young, they enjoyed "dressing up" in this memento from so long ago.

When classes were changing, it was a custom at our school for the boys to ask to carry your books down the hall from one class to another. I remember two certain boys who would race to see who could carry my books. All the while my boyfriend was standing at the end of the hall watching. I would come into class fuming and complaining to my girlfriend that my boyfriend saw who was carrying my books. She would say, "Oh, Mary, stop complaining! You have to be flattered. I wish someone would ask to carry my books for me!" Later, she wrote in my yearbook, "Boys are bothersome but I like being bothered!" I don't think many boys ask to carry a girl's books nowadays.

Having a major part in our senior school play holds special memories for me. In one scene of the play, I wore a long, white gown and danced on stage with the class president. It was a special scene since in real life, he did have a crush on me. When time for the prom came, even though I was going to the prom with someone else, this class president had a beautiful orchid corsage delivered to my house the night of our senior prom. That boy, who is now a retired brigadier general, will never know how special I felt and what a thrill it was to receive that orchid. You must remember that back then, orchids were more expensive and very rare. I still have the orchid pressed in a scrapbook along with the very pretty red carnations I wore.

There are sad school remembrances also. I remember a sad time for my younger sister, Flo. Her high school sweetheart, Barkley, was a great person and played on the football and basketball teams. Flo was a cheerleader and after a football game he took her home and left about 11:00 p.m. Early the following morning two friends came to our house and told us the sad news that Barkley had been killed the night before in a car accident on his way home. Barkley's neck was broken. People thought he may have been injured in the football game which could have caused the accident. I'm sure it took Flo many years to get over that high school tragedy. Many wondered why it happened and it took a long time for folks to move past the sadness of his death. He was only sixteen.

Siler City High School Dance
(Mary—first row, second right)

Old MacDonald's Farm and the Pony Tale

Sister Frances and Tricksy

Our farm had horses, cows, chickens, pigs, goats, and at one time or another almost every pet imaginable. Squirrels, crows, rabbits, and even pigs were turned into pets as well as the usual host of dogs and cats.

One of our favorites was a bulldog named Junie. He was so ugly that people passing by would avoid him at all cost if possible. Truth was, he was completely harmless! Our most favorite pet was a white Eskimo spitz named Tricksy. He did tricks for food. In later years, Mama had a Dalmatian named Cindy who was very protective. We always needed to watch that dog. She would bite certain people.

Some of our cats were barn cats. They caught the mice that ate the corn that went in the barn that fed the cows that gave the milk that fed the cats! A limerick or what? The barn cats thought they were in cat heaven. Sleeping in the hay loft, they were lurking nearby when we milked the cows each morning and night. They scampered into the cow stall for a bowl of fresh, warm milk straight from the cow.

I remember Mama straining the milk through cheesecloth before it was ready to drink. Milk from our farm was never pasteurized and we were seldom sick. Our milk was wonderfully rich tasting and probably packed with nutrients since our cows ate pasture grass and were fed hay and corn with no antibiotics or hormones. But the milk was not always rich tasting. Each spring one of our pastures had fennel (a bitter weed) come up and we had to shut that pasture off from the cows. When they ate the fennel, their milk tasted bitter as well. Not harmful but we couldn't drink that bitter milk!

There were chickens for eggs as well as good ole' country fried chicken. A daily chore was gathering the fresh eggs from the nests. Occasionally at night we would hear the chickens making a loud alarming clucking sound. Often, it was discovered that a predator, a weasel or a black snake, was nearby so the story about the fox in the henhouse is true!

Our chicken eggs were probably more nutritious than today since they were free range chickens and raised without stress hormones and antibiotics. Chickens laid their eggs in a nest. We hatched chicks from some of those eggs. But there were natural predators after everything on the farm. Hawks swooped down and tried to catch the baby chicks. The mother hen clucked loudly and the chicks hid under her outstretched wings for protection. A large windmill helped scare the hawks away, but not entirely!

Free range chickens are today considered by natural food stores as healthier because of the crowded conditions that other hot house chickens are grown in. They release stress hormones and are given antibiotics which are passed on to us. Oh! For the simple life again.… There are more than a few good things to be said for growing up on a farm. New food concepts today, but not to us; free range and pasture fed was everyday to us. We also had colorful bantam roosters and speckled guinea hens. The guineas were more like wild birds and hid their nests in the honeysuckle patches along the pasture fences at the edge of the woods. Guineas have a rounded shape with dark grey feathers spotted with white. They make a loud piercing sound when disturbed or frightened and are loners, preferring to stay in our pasture area and travel in their own group. Beautiful but strange birds! The roosters woke us in the early morning. I shall never forget when I was in the fourth grade and the teacher asked the smartest kid in the class what a rooster was. He did not know and I thought that was a real cock-a-doo-dle-doo boo boo! He was a city kid and did not know anything about farm life. I felt so superior because the roosters were our alarm clocks every day.

The thing I recall most vividly about the chickens was watching Mama wringing their necks and seeing the headless bodies jump around for a few minutes. Some people chopped the heads off. I was too "chicken" to do either, but sure did enjoy that country fried chicken. After the chicken stopped jumping, it was dipped in scalding water and de-feathered, singed with a flame to burn the down feathers off. The feet, legs and entrails were removed. It was then cut up (as we see them in the market today) and ready to be fried.

We owned a mischievous farm pony named Jake. He was so mean and bucked two of my nephews off, breaking one of the boys' arms. Jake probably did not like two people on his back at one time so he just decided to get rid of that heavy load!

Every time Mama went into the barnyard to gather eggs or do other chores, Jake

One of the barns on the old farm as it looks today

would follow her around. If she did not have an apple or sugar for him, he would nip and try to bite her. He was only trying to get her attention but she just didn't like that pesky pony! I really don't remember what happened to old Jake, but I think another home was found for him where he could continue his winsome ways. At least, until one discovered the truth about Jake and probably shipped him off to another unsuspecting person. Perhaps he found a good home and reformed from his pesky pony ways.

We had a beautiful but spirited horse that liked to run. I didn't realize as I was riding him that one click of the tongue would send him into a full gallop. All I could do was hang on for dear life as he took me on a wild ride through low hanging branches and finally back to the barn gate and stopped! A spirited horse indeed! I haven't been riding since! I should have gotten right back on that horse and conquered my fear of riding.

Healthy Choices and Chicken Soup

We were seldom sick growing up, probably due to a combination of fresh air, clean water, home grown food and just the simple life. I never remember being sick and going to the doctor as we had various home remedies including Mama's chicken soup. Our beloved family doctor came to our home when new babies arrived. When we broke a bone, off to the doctor we went.

With a large family, bones were broken, at one time or another, climbing trees, walking off roofs or falling off benches (that was me!). My siblings and I were adventurous and unafraid too. I remember when my sister Flo was watching some hunters on our property and promptly walked off the roof and broke her wrist. Once I was dancing on a bench and fell off. I broke and twisted my arm, discovering I had landed on a rock.

Mama called Daddy to come home and get my arm set. He came to pick me up and looked up into those two hundred year old oak trees in our yard and said "If anybody else up there wants to jump and break something, go ahead now and I'll take you with Mary." He had a real sense of humor! At the time, though, I didn't think it was quite so funny.

Before my arm was set, I was put to sleep by inhaling ether. The surgeon who set my arm instructed me to carry a pail of sand around to help straighten my arm. This lasted for 2 to 3 weeks. That bucket of sand was very heavy!

Today, setting a bone is quite different. My daughter-in-law, Tina, who is a physician, will be amused no doubt by the prescription—Carry a bucket of sand! But you know, it worked! I can just envision Tina telling patients to carry a bucket of sand to help straighten a broken arm. Can you imagine the look on their faces as they run out of her office exclaiming "there's a crazy doctor in there!"

Colds, stomach aches, and other ailments were sometimes treated with various home remedies such as paregoric, honey and vinegar, Vicks Vapor Rub, camphor ice dissolved in corn liquor and castor oil (Yuk!). But the most remembered—chicken soup! Even today chicken soup is highly recommended for treating colds. Wouldn't Dr. Mama be pleased to know she was ahead of her time! That's called wisdom.

A ten year study, just out, found that organic food is much higher in nutritional value than traditional foods that are not organic certified.

Today, there is a trend toward natural alternatives in medicine as well as foods without the unhealthy additives in so much of our food. One major complaint is that organic food is more expensive. On the other hand, it may be a matter of who you pay. More for organic grown food or more for doctor bills? We improve our health by eating healthy foods. I think it is worth the extra cost!

Doctors are life savers in many cases but I want to also take greater responsibility for my own health and well being. I think eating healthy is a major factor in staying healthy.

Summer Fun and City Cousins

During summer vacations our cousins, Nancy and Dot Clark, visited from Raleigh, North Carolina to experience farm life, ride horses and help out on the farm. They especially enjoyed gathering and eating fresh figs from two huge fig trees in the back yard. In later years, Nancy and Dot came back to the farm each year without fail to visit and gather figs. I'm sure they came to recapture earlier times on the farm and to experience family and to connect with those pleasant summertime memories, such as wading in the clear cool creek on a hot summer day.

My sister Margaret and cousin Nancy

Visiting my Grandfather Lambert's farm was an enjoyable late summer memory. They had a huge arbor covered with scuppernong grapes. We gathered and ate the grapes and also enjoyed eating mulberries from a large tree in their front yard. We had purple tongues and fingers after that experience.

On warm summer nights, we played games outside like "Ain't no bears out tonight." The front porch light was on and the front steps served as home base. Everyone hid behind the trees and shrubs in the yard. The "hunter" leaving home base ventured out to tag whoever he or she could find before someone could touch home base and be home free. Mama and Daddy often sat on the porch and watched with interest who would be tagged. Sometimes Daddy would help someone to get to home base. If we were nearby, he would whisper "run" so we could beat the "hunter" to base. One night our neighbor Catherine collided with one of my brothers and got a huge "hen egg" on her forehead. That ended our fun for the night....

We did the usual things like catching fireflies at night and putting them into jars to see the magic up close. Children still enjoy catching fireflies. Rocks were thrown in the air and the bats swooped down to intercept them believing they were insects. On sunny days, bumblebees were caught in jars. Of course, we were regularly stung by honeybees when running barefoot through the clover. We avoided or at least were very careful handling box turtles and terrapins. We were told if they snapped and bit they wouldn't let go until it thundered. This worked as we were never snapped!

Fun was catching June bugs, tying a long thread to their leg and releasing them to buzz around. We tried to see how many we could have flying around at one time. No harm was done. They were released to fly away to be caught another day.

The boys played with marbles, made and walked on stilts (tom walkers), carved and shot slingshots (bean shooters) and of course, yo-yo's. There was a ball field in the pasture where the neighbors would gather on weekends to play ball. The Dowd, Burns, and Siler Families all came and later everyone, hot and tired, would swim in the nearby creek. There was no television then and it was probably a good thing. Today, television may be for young children too much mindless entertainment. Psychologists are confirming more attention deficit disorders among children who watch television for hours at a time, as well as contributing to the epidemic of obesity and juvenile diabetes among the young.

My sister Flo and I made mud pies, built playhouses and played with the dolls we got each Christmas. Speaking of dirt, the latest pediatric information is that children are too clean and not exposed enough to natural organisms in the soil so have more incidence of asthma and other illnesses and less natural immunity. We played in the dirt everyday so perhaps that is the reason we were seldom sick! Florence and I are the two youngest and only two years apart so we grew up together and shared more experiences.

Sweet gum trees grew in abundance on the farm and as kids, we enjoyed our own home-grown chewing gum by harvesting rosin from cuts made in the trees. It had a rubber-like consistency and tasted not quite as good as some of today's chewing gum but we were inventive and the more we chewed the better it got! Sweet gum rosin was used for medicinal purposes so it was probably good for us. Half the fun was the creative process of finding and extracting the gum from our own trees.

It is hard to imagine what a quarter could buy in the 1930's and 1940's. My brother, Ted, recalls spending his quarter one Fourth of July—ten cents for a movie, five cents for a bag of peanuts, and five cents for candy at Sharpes Store. There were lots of good candy to be had—Mary Janes and BB Bats for a nickel each and many more of the old fashioned favorites. I guess you could say those really were the good ole days!

On Saturday nights neighbors were invited over to play the card game Rook and sometimes checkers. The Fields family and the Moore family usually came and my daddy and their dad would play two of the children. They sometimes were caught signaling and nudging each other under the table to gain advantage. What rascals they were! The adults can be forgiven for their little cheating episodes since it was done with a sense of competitive fun and fellowship—a time for family and friends to be together.

Our mothers talked and visited while they played and later refreshments were served. This included popcorn, homemade chocolate fudge all served with coffee or lemonade in the summertime but the best was Mama's chocolate pie!

Mama's Chocolate Pie Recipe

For the filling:

1 cup sugar	1 ½ cups milk
4 tbsp. cocoa	1 tsp. vanilla
4 tbsp. flour	2 tbsp. butter

2 egg yolks, save the whites for meringue

Mix sugar, cocoa, and flour. Add milk and 2 egg yolks, beaten. Cook over medium heat, stirring until thickened. Remove from heat. Add vanilla and butter. Pour into baked pie shell. Top with meringue and brown (See below for meringue recipe.)

Mama's Meringue

2 egg whites
1 tsp. vanilla
4 tbsp. sugar
¼ tsp. cream of tartar

Beat the egg whites, sugar, vanilla, and cream of tartar until stiff. Cover the pie filling and brown at 375 degrees.

Summer Storms and Old Time Remedies

After a hot day, the summer rains came and cooled everything down. We often went on the front porch, wrapped in a cozy quilt and sat in a rocking chair and listened to the gentle raindrops falling on the tin roof. A soothing sound you don't soon forget. Especially the night rains as our upstairs bedrooms were near the tin roof. If that did not put one to sleep, nothing ever would!

Storms were a different story. When thunderstorms came with thunder and lightning, Mama would make everyone come into the living room and sit quietly until the storm was over. It was as though she was showing respect for the fury of the storm and respect for God.

Once, my Daddy decided to stay on the front porch during a particularly loud storm. I have to tell you, he wasn't afraid of the devil himself. A lightning bolt practically knocked him out of his rocking chair striking only a few feet away. That brought him inside promptly. He bolted out of that rocking chair almost as quick as the lightning and remarked on the way in "Damn, that was close." He respected the weather a lot more after that episode!

All the children enjoyed wading in the swiftly running streams in our pasture after a "gully washer" of a summer storm. Our pastures were pleasant places for us. One was where the killdeer birds nested in the rocks. They made a lovely sound and we looked for their speckled eggs among the rocks. The mother bird would fly off her nest and fake a broken wing to get our attention away from the babies.

Another summertime fun was catching pollywogs or tadpoles in the pasture pond and watching them develop legs. They have gills and a long tail before becoming pond frogs. We were fascinated also by the water striders skimming along the waters surface.

There was a small pond in the pasture. While swimming one hot summer day, we got out of the water and saw three snake heads poke up out of the water or what we thought were snake heads—they may have been turtles. We thought that everyone had been swimming with snakes! I don't know how we all survived so well on that farm.

While running around the farm, we stepped on rusty nails and such but seldom got sick or badly hurt. When we stepped on a nail, the remedy was to pour kerosene or turpentine on the cut and wrap it with a piece of fatback. That would either cure anything or kill you! I doubt there is medical evidence to support that particular prescription, but it worked! We were told the salty bacon and kerosene drew the poison out and killed harmful germs. No one ever got lockjaw from the rusty nails so perhaps some of the old remedies did work contrary to popular opinion today.

Wounds from foot punctures were treated by smoking the wound with the fumes of sugar placed on hot coals. If a wound got infected, soaking it frequently in a solution of Epsom salts and hot water was almost always effective in preventing blood poisoning.

There were poisonous snakes all around but we were never bitten. There must have been a guiding force or guardian angels around us. I am truly thankful that we did not experience any deaths or tragedies like so many other families did and many of our ancestors as well.

The Gathering Spot

Our large front porch, filled with rocking chairs and a swing, was often the gathering place. We would shell butterbeans, snap green beans or just talk, listen, and enjoy the cool breeze after a hot summer day! There were nightly sounds of frogs in the pond, tree frogs, cicadas, crickets, whippoorwills and bobwhites calling their mates. Daddy would often sit on the porch and call up the night singers by imitating their call perfectly. They would get closer and closer to the house as he answered their call.

Sometimes a steam engine would stop at a nearby small community called Ore Hill. There the engine would fill up with water from a large tank. Even though Ore Hill was about two miles away, in the stillness of a hot summer night with the windows open, we could hear the old steamer start puffing away up the track.

Everything was beautiful at dusk as the sun set and reflected in the golden pond. I remember so many beautiful sunsets. At dusk, what fun to look for toad frogs and, of course, chase lightning bugs. The things seen every day like the toads are more of a rare occurrence now as well as honeybees and other insects. Their population has been greatly reduced from spraying insecticides with reckless abandon. Hopefully, we will use more natural means to reduce the number of unwanted ones that may be a threat to crops. The good insects are sometimes killed along with the bad.

I think all should take greater responsibility for the environment before our eco-system is in real trouble. There is only one planet to sustain us as far as we now know.

Country Summers

Country summers with skies
of azure blue
The green grass sparkles
Like diamonds with morning dew.

Twilight grows bright
as roosters awaken the day
And crow the night away
in just their special way.

Billowing clouds of cotton quietly sail aloft,
so soft as kittens' feet
Morning walks along a laughing
babbling brook bring joy complete.

Nesting birds carry secrets
None of us can know or see.
Their joyful song fill our souls
With infinite love and immortality.

Country summers with wonders
and wellness so abundant.
Everything's alive and bathed
in beauty; beckoning us to truly trust
in love above.

Mary Elkins Cheek

Scary Times

As we were sleeping one hot, balmy summer night, a very scary incident occurred. The windows were open to let in the fresh air when a large, black dog came onto the porch. He jumped against the window screen and got into the house. Daddy was awakened, got up and hit the dog on the head with a fire poker. He thought the dog was dead and threw it out the back door thinking we would dispose of it when morning came. The next morning, the dog was gone! He had only knocked the dog unconscious. No one ever knew from whence it came nor where it went since we never saw the dog again. A true scary time for us.

Another frightening time as well as a vivid memory occurred when a forest fire threatened to burn across our property. The orange fiery glow lit up the night sky behind the tree-lined forest. What an eerie sight! Our whole family was out in the yard watching it advance closer and closer. As I was a young child then, this was especially frightening. My brothers were summoned to help fight the fire late into the night. They came back exhausted and black from the fire and smoke. Fortunately, it never reached our property but was beaten back and finally extinguished. Fire trucks weren't available to fight fires in the country at that time. Our family and neighbors fought the fires with large green branches. That forest fire was thought to have started from the highway when someone tossed a cigarette. Countless forest fires have been started from cigarettes being thrown carelessly from vehicles.

Each year during the summer months, we had chimney swifts nesting in the chimney. Chimney swifts are dark-colored birds with long narrow wings and a short tail. We heard the baby swifts chirping and saw the adult birds flying in and out of the top of the chimney gathering food for their young. One morning Mama came into the living room and there on the hearth was a black snake. It had climbed up the side of the chimney hunting for the baby birds and had fallen down onto the hearth. Needless to say, it was promptly killed and removed along with the chimney swifts. Snakes are great climbers—especially hungry ones!

Rabid dogs were a regular spring occurrence. One beautiful morning my sister Florence and I were playing in the yard. Mama ran out and warned us of a mad dog, which was what we called a rabid dog, spotted down the road coming our way. A neighbor had phoned to warn us. Flo and I were frightened and quickly ran for the nearest safe place and climbed onto the woodhouse roof. That particular dog was killed before it reached our place. In all the excitement, they forgot about us on the woodhouse roof. Unfortunately we could not get down and had to call for help.

Early one morning about 5:00 a.m., we were all sleeping. Suddenly, my brother, Jack, awoke and heard our two pet pigs squealing loudly in the backyard. He got out of bed and ran into the yard. He saw a dog attacking our pet pigs and was able to beat the dog off them. Jack went back to bed. Later that morning we got the word that a rabid dog had been killed at the neighbor's house up the way. It was the one that had been in our yard. Jack was so fortunate not to have been attacked and bitten! Indeed, a lucky brother that morning. Someone must have been praying for us or our guardian angels were on patrol. Unfortunately, our two pet pigs were not so lucky. They had to be put down as a result of scratches and bites. Our little pet terrier dog had to be put down also for fear that he had gotten in contact with a rabid dog as he was in the yard. They were buried along the hedgerows. We were forbidden to go near the graves for fear of coming in contact with rabies.

In those days, people especially feared those rabid dogs. Part of the reason was from the stories we were told about how long and painful the treatment for rabies was. Large shot needles were used in the stomach area over a period of several days. I shudder to think how close Jack came to experiencing the pain of those treatments.

Rabid dogs are rare today, but there are increasing incidents of rabid wild animals coming in contact with humans as their habitat is shrinking. Foxes, raccoons, possums and bats are just a few that may carry rabies.

Mystery Plants and Hidden Secrets

There were many plants found on our farm. Some carried hidden secrets. Our mystery plants were large, beautiful plants with trumpet-shaped purple flowers only known as "those 'ole Jimson weeds." These plants came up each year in the barn area and in the pig pens. None of us knew the seed pods contained narcotic hallucinogenic properties. We were only told they were poisonous! The pods were prickly and contained little black seeds.

Another hidden secret was found in abundance in our pastures. They were filled with what is commonly called "shrooms" today. These were little mushrooms that grew in our pastures in cow patties. Imagine that! We sometimes accidentally stepped in those cow patties and mushrooms barefoot! Yuk! They apparently have hallucinogenic properties also. I'm not sure our parents knew why they were "poisonous." They never revealed the secret if they did.

The drug culture today would have literally been in hog heaven on our farm, especially in the hog pen! I'm grateful we were not aware of these plants' medicinal properties. We may have been tempted to take some "out of this world" trips. I still wonder if our parents knew full well what those little black seeds contained as well as the little mushrooms. If so, wise parents they were!

A word of caution. My son, John, related how he knew two people at his school who ate the little seeds and shrooms, overdosed and almost died. They ended up in the hospital unconscious. A word to the wise—don't even try it!

Rich City Mice and Poor Country Cousins

My Aunt Beta and Uncle Luther Britt came to visit occasionally from Lumberton, North Carolina. It reminded me of the story about the rich city mice and their poor country cousins. The moral of which was that the poor country cousins were not as poor as I thought.

Uncle Luther was a prominent criminal attorney and Aunt Beta had been director of nurses at a large hospital. They had many honors and their three children, in turn, became lawyers and one became a doctor. One was so highly intelligent that she entered Duke University in Durham, North Carolina at age 16. Luther Junior served four terms in the state senate as well as chairman of the Judiciary Committee. He was Lumberton's City Attorney for twelve years. He was State President of the North Carolina Jaycees and served as the national director. He was appointed to many state study commissions by several governors. Unfortunately, he died of a massive heart attack at the young age of 46. Had he lived longer, I am sure he would have achieved much more. His son, a lawyer, serves as Roberson County District Attorney. I always admired their down to earth attitudes in spite of the obvious advantages they enjoyed.

As a little girl, I was intimidated by that but later realized we were also rich in many other ways. Poor perhaps by some standards but I never felt poor at all. The advantages of growing up on our farm and the good health we enjoyed as well as the everyday lessons of life were also valuable. I feel the many good things we received from our growing up years as well as our heredity have contributed greatly to our longevity. We are all still here and my oldest sister, Margaret, is approaching 82 years of age.

We just learned to "roll with the punches," and "take an old, cold tater and wait" and had just plain toughness to survive in our world today. Living in a family of seven children and two parents precludes being selfish or self-centered. I believe these are worthwhile values we carry with us forever and character building traits for sure.

It really isn't what happens to us in life, but how we respond. Remember, God is never the author of suffering in the world, and will sustain us and be there for us through anything. He, in His wisdom, sometimes allows things for our ultimate spiritual growth and we learn to depend on Him.

Health History

Recording family health history has important advantages in determining risk factors for many inherited diseases such as diabetes and breast cancer that can be passed to subsequent generations. Being proactive when there are hereditary factors concerning specific health issues that can pass from one generation to another may help save lives. Promoting healthy lifestyles and using preventive measures where risk factors are known could prevent the occurrence of some diseases or make them more manageable.

Our family health history is important for future generations. Generally, we have not had a lot of hereditary illnesses on the Elkins or Lambert sides of the family.

Most Elkins family members died of heart attacks as did my father and all his siblings. There was no cancer or diabetes in the family, as far as I know, although today that does not necessarily apply as there are so many things in our environment that predispose us to these diseases.

Daddy may have had a condition called Myasthenia Gravis. It is a rare disease with no known cure. I do not know if it is hereditary. This happened late in life after he retired. The symptoms are weakness in the eyelids causing them to droop and the throat muscles are eventually affected making it hard to swallow. Weakness in other areas of the body can occur. Paralysis of the heart muscles follows. He took medication for this in order to swallow better. He eventually died suddenly of a heart attack or stroke at age 64. Myasthenia Gravis may have contributed to this.

Grandfather Lambert lived a long life to the age of 88 as well as my mother, who lived to be 92. After a series of strokes, she died a year or two later.

Sleep Walkers: Asleep and Awake

At least on one occasion while we were growing up, my oldest brother, Jim, was a sleepwalker. One particular night he woke his younger brother Ted and explained that the house was on fire. He led Ted down the stairs and out the door. Ted was awake but did not realize Jim was sleepwalking.

My mom awoke and heard footsteps coming down the stairs and rushed out in the hall to see what was going on. Ted said, "The house is on fire and we are getting out!" Jim led Ted down the back steps and out into the yard insisting the house was on fire. My mom replied "Where is the fire? I don't see any fire!" She immediately realized Jim was sleepwalking and told them in no uncertain terms to go back to bed. They obeyed but evidently Jim was never fully awake. I think Ted was probably totally confused as he was wide awake during the entire episode. This sleepwalking story has been told many times over the years. I hope I got it right and Jim doesn't mind reading about it one more time.

A person can be semi-asleep and capable of following instructions but not able to remember later what happened. There have been textbook examples of persons doing all sorts of things over a period of time and not remembering anything about it.

Balancing Love, Work, Play and Discipline

There were many great and wonderful experiences growing up on the farm, but I realized that we also encountered negative experiences. As I began writing these reflections, I realized our family did not express emotions very well. I always knew our parents loved us but I suppose simply rearing seven children and providing for our needs was a feat in itself and I will always be grateful. We were fortunate not to experience any terrible tragedies as others did. However, our parents seldom displayed their emotional side.

Their attitude was a no nonsense, get the job done position. It seemed as though if you showed outward emotions you were weak. Just keep a stiff upper lip like the English. Well, our ancestors did come from England ...

I found it hard to express emotions even when appropriate. This could be seen as a sign of being strong, but I realize it was repressed emotions and how I grew up. I feel all my siblings would agree we were affected to some degree by this lack of outward expression. Maybe families of long ago were much like that. They wanted us to be tough and survive in the world. Some of this may be desirable but we found it hard to communicate positive feelings. We could express negative emotions—scrapping with each other as well as anyone but it would have been nice to have been encouraged to say "I love you" more. As I have grown older, my advice would be to discipline with love and express your feelings of care and love for family and others. Being a great person is when you unselfishly give to others in words and deeds. We all need to express our emotions freely and not be repressed or embarrassed to say "I love you."

Our parents probably thought we needed to be tough to survive since their lives had been so affected by the Great Depression. They parented the way they were parented. We were told how our Grandfather Elkins, who experienced the harsh post Civil War reconstruction period, made all the children work so hard that even on rainy days when they could not work in the fields they were often made to pick up rocks or pull weeds along fence lines. The children were not allowed to go to bed at night without filling their shoes with cotton seed. They had to pick a shoe full of seeds from the cotton by hand. Later cotton gins extracted the seed. He was a large cotton farmer which was a labor intensive enterprise as well as most other tasks on the farm in those days. Every day was a full working day except for Sunday, the Fourth of July and Christmas Day. It was said that he made everyone around him walk the straight and narrow by working the "devil out of them." However, none worked harder than he did.

Families were tough and self-sufficient. An example is the story of Lizzie, one of the children, accidentally cutting off four fingers while chopping wood. Grandmother Elkins picked the fingers up out of the chips, cleaned them off, and sewed them back on with a regular needle and cotton thread which, in my mind, is an amazing account of strength and determination. Immediate self-help action was called for; the doctor was four miles away by horseback. All but one of Lizzie's fingers were saved. She later chose nursing as a lifetime career. I often wonder if this incident may have been a factor in her choice of professions.

People had to be self-sufficient and I am sure that any sign of emotion was considered a weakness. It is unfortunate that they did not have more balance in their lives. I believe the notion of all work and very little play caused one of the children to become the "black sheep" of the family.

Our Uncle Durham was a very intelligent person. When he was in school and was not paying attention during a math lesson, the teacher reprimanded him. He replied, "There is not one problem in that math book that I can't solve." She challenged him and he won. I would imagine that he might have been bored with the lesson since there were no accelerated classes. He never worked at a real job because he stated his father worked everyone to death on the farm and he was not going to "strike a lick at a snake" for the rest of his life and after a certain time he didn't. It seemed his choices were a direct result of a life-long bitterness or rebellion toward his father; from having too much discipline and not enough outward demonstration of love. Being an infantry "doughboy" on the front lines and in the trenches in France during much of World War I as well as never knowing his real mother probably contributed to his profound negative attitude toward life.

After returning from WWI, Durham spent much of the rest of his life making a good living at gambling and winning with some of the wealthier people in town. He owned land and traded horses. At one time, he owned an airplane and the local airstrip. He lived by his wits and the ability to gamble and win. He certainly led a self-centered life. Uncle Durham died having never married on March 2, 1960 of heart problems at the age of 64.

Our negative experiences, regrets and mistakes should make us better, not bitter. We choose, not realizing that we actually only have today. Yesterday is gone. Tomorrow may never come, so live each day for others. It's only in giving our lives away that we find our purpose. Dying to self and living a Christ centered life, to me, is the ultimate expression of a life well lived. Only then can we know why we are here in the first place. To be free from the tyranny of self is freedom indeed! It's life more abundantly here and hereafter. It is peace, joy and rest to fulfill the purpose for which you were created.

In the final analysis, we all have to make choices about the kind of lives we live. I think Uncle Durham's life was a tragedy and not lived to its fullest.

Horse Sense
"You can lead a horse to water but you can't make him drink"

I have vivid memories as this expression was played out every day on the farm. After a day of working in the fields or plowing the garden, the horses or mules were unhitched from the wagon or plow. The bridle was left on and they were led or ridden through the lane and down a path to the spring fed watering hole in the pasture to drink. They generally drank large amounts of water. Sometimes, when the animals had done only light work, they would just stand there and no one could make them drink. The quotation, "You can lead a horse to water, but you can't make him drink", was probably inspired by the daily practice of taking the horses to the watering hole.

This applies to our lives also. We can be taken to the water, but it's our final decision whether we choose to drink or not. Our choices, paths taken, decisions made, ultimately depend on where one ends up in this life and, I believe, the next.

Snapshots of Farm Memories

Raising the Roof

When we were children, many happy hours were spent building tunnels with bales of straw housed in our barn made of logs. It was one of our favorite places to play especially on rainy days with the raindrops falling gently on the tin roof. Inside there were ladders on each end for climbing into the loft area, which was a really inviting place for young children. The loft had bales of straw and hay. It was a neat place to play until our father discovered we were building tunnels and "raised the roof" about getting suffocated from the bales collapsing in on us and put a stop to our fun, for that day anyway.

Strong Nails—A Child's Remedy

My youngest sister, Florence, recalls when she was a small child, fertilizer was being spread in the corn fields. She asked our father what this was and he explained it was used to make the corn grow faster and stronger. She buried her little fingers into the fertilizer thinking it would make her nails grow quickly long and strong. Of course, that was not a very good idea. Fertilizer will not make your nails grow faster but what an innocent farm memory of a child so long ago ...

Gone Fishing

Using a hook, line, and red cork sinker along with a bamboo pole, fishing in the nearby creek was summer fun. We caught small minnows and colorful sun perch. Fishing worms were dug from the rich black earth behind the barn. The black compost was teeming with fishing worms and we filled a jar with worms and a bit of dirt. With our jar of worms and bamboo poles slung over our shoulders, a fishin' we would go.

We searched for crayfish under the rocks and played in the streams, walking in the cool water on hot summer days.

The little babbling brook also had leeches. A leech is a worm that lives in the water. They would quickly attach themselves to our feet so we had to be vigilant about pulling them off. Leeches today are used to save lives and heal wounds. Are not all God's creatures here for a purpose?

A Quarter Bribe

Two or three cows had to be milked twice daily. My sister Florence recalls our brother Jack bribing her to milk the cows when it was his turn by paying her twenty-five cents to do this for him. He wanted to go somewhere and didn't want to take his turn so he talked Flo into milking the cows for him for a mere quarter—a real bargain even back then!

The Traveling Salesman

Everyone looked forward to seeing the Raleigh Man, a traveling salesman that came to sell vanilla flavoring, candy and many bottled products. He sold our favorite candy, a rectangular shaped coconut bar with pink, white and brown stripes. I still look for that candy bar but have not been able to find it anywhere. I'm sure country markets may still sell it. So-oo good!

Swing High, Swing Low

My oldest sister, Margaret, remembers babysitting my youngest sister Florence when she was only a few months old. She was on a pillow in the swing and Margaret was swinging her a little too high when the pillow slid out and the baby with it! Fortunately, Florence landed in the shrubbery and, thankfully, the pillow cushioned the fall and she was unhurt. A scare Margaret never forgot!

Brave Little Lad

My brother Jim remembers an interesting story and scary time going to the grist mill with our farm hand. The grist mill was where wheat and corn were ground into flour and corn meal. He was about five years old when they were ready to return home and the man who was with Jim saw some friends and disappeared leaving him alone with the horses and wagon. When the farm hand didn't return, Jim drove the team of horses and wagon several miles back home. A brave thing for a five year old but he arrived back safely. An adventure never to be forgotten and needless to say, the hired hand was never heard from again and a good thing that was!

Another Narrow Escape

Jim recalls taking younger brother Ted about four miles from home to the river to fish. He had a large hatchet in his belt. Jim was attempting to carry Ted across a briar patch on his back when Ted's leg was badly cut by the hatchet as he jumped on Jim's back. Jim carried him four miles back home. Mama immediately called Daddy home, as she often did with all the broken bones, etc. Daddy drove Ted to Siler City to the doctor's office. Apparently, this doctor never gave Ted anything for pain and commenced to sew up the wound with cat gut and a needle. Ted remarked "that smarted!" No wonder they referred to the doctor as "the butcher." Today, a lawsuit for malpractice would surely ensue. I believe there is a time to live and a time to die. We are really only here for a short time. Let's make good use of it!

A Free Fish Tale

Brother Ted told about a fishing trip at nearby Meadow Creek. They would use a seine, which is a large, weighted fishing net, in the river to catch fish. This particular day a snake was spotted coming from under a log in the creek with a large catfish in its mouth. Somehow they were able to get that big fish in their seine and the snake lost its meal and we had catfish for supper!

Little Green Apples

After a hard morning of working in the fields under the hot summer sun, it was often a custom of farm hands to take a break and rest after the big noontime meal.

Sometimes they would sleep or rest under one of our huge shady oaks or most often on a bench under the shelter in the barn area. As young children, we would gather little green apples from our orchard and sneak around to the shelter, throw the green apples and run as fast as possible before they realized what had happened or who did it. They woke up threatening to get even; not knowing exactly who did it and, of course, we all acted puzzled about what they were talking about. (A skillful tactic employed to  get away with our dirty little deed). Innocent fun but not nearly as inventive as others we heard about.

Other farm hands went to sleep only to wake up with red pepper on their lips! Green apples wouldn't hold a candle to that prank! When they woke up, they had more than hot lips. They were "hot under the collar" with some hot words as well.

We were children just having fun until Mama found out and put a stop to it, threatening to use her green switch on our mischievous backsides.

Not M & M's

Our children always enjoyed visiting the farm and seeing the animals. Once our two youngest children, John and Laurie, went into the pasture where the cows were grazing. They each has a bag of M & M candy.

The cows spotted them and came charging toward them, thinking, I suppose, they were going to feed them. Our frightened children started throwing their candy to the cows, hoping to escape. They ran for the nearest fence and scampered over to safety. They were only 5 and 8 years old and were much more cautious after that, although, the cows, I'm sure, meant no harm. They only wanted food—but not M & M candy!

Treasures from Home

I have gathered a few things from the old farm that hold precious memories for me. A very old oil lamp, flat black irons and my bed from home are some of my special treasures. My bed is a very old brass and iron bed. I still sleep in that bed and will someday pass it on to my daughter who loves antiques. It will become a family keepsake. I  have a few old pottery jugs that held all that cider and vinegar we made and a special candlestick. A treasure indeed is the gold coin stickpin my dad always wore in his tie.

I have a Home Sweet Home needlepoint picture. No one knows exactly when it was made, but my mother thought it belonged to her grandmother's mother. What a special gift to be passed on to future generations.

I still enjoy collecting antiques that remind me of bygone days of my farm home. I collect telephone insulators like the ones that were on our line as well as cobalt blue bottles and other antique bottles and jars. I have a special single tree with hooks that hold copper molds in our kitchen that came from the farm. A single tree was used to hitch the horses to a plow. I see all these things and go back in time for a little visit and a flood of memories!

Other family members have special treasures from the farm. Margaret has Dad's violin and a special butter mold. My brother Jack, who later become Sheriff of Chatham County as our father was before him, has Dad's guns, holsters, Masonic ring and blackjack (a leather-covered metal piece used to subdue those resisting arrest). Today,  tasers or pepper spray are used instead. He has some special tools that were used for Model T. Ford cars. All have pictures and other mementos. My cousin, Dot, has the glass door china closet where the delicious cakes Mama baked were kept at Christmas. Sister Frances has an exquisite antique cut-glass water pitcher that belonged to my mother's family. My cousin, Nancy, has a unique antique hunt board. This was used in our dining room. It has back legs that are shorter than the front for drainage after hunts. All are treasured memories of home.

PART II

Parents and Beloved Lulee

Other Memories From Home

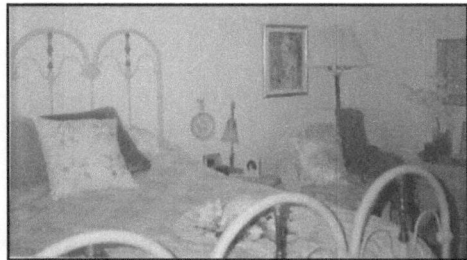

Above: My bed from home.

Right: A table from the old home place.

Glassware and pottery from the farm

Memories of Daddy—His gold coin stickpin and his violin.

My Parents—Alma Joy Elkins
and Tatum Thomas Elkins

My parents were born and grew up within a few miles of each other in the Siler City area of Chatham County, North Carolina. The two family farms joined so they had known each other and went to school together.

My mother, Alma Joy Lambert Elkins, was the youngest in her family of two sisters, Rena and Bertha and brother, Oscar. Oscar remained at the home place with his wife, Luta White Lambert and their two sons, Bobby and Joe Lambert who cared for my grandfather until his death at age 88.

 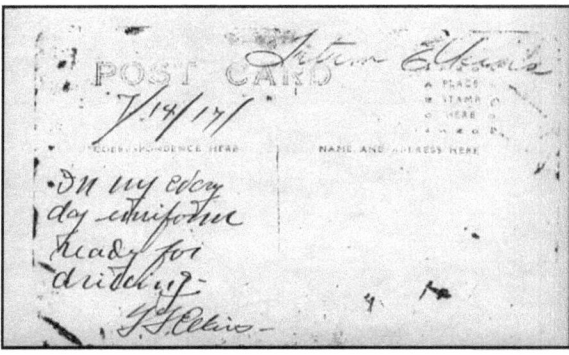

Postcard photograph sent to Mom from our Father while in boot camp in New Jersey, July 14, 1917. The card reads: In my everyday uniform ready for drilling.

After Dad came home from the Navy, they were married on March 2, 1923 and moved into the home where we all grew up. This home place of 150 acres was inherited by my mother from her uncle, Frank Jones.

Both of my parents lost their mothers at a young age. Mom was only two years old when her mother, Lula Hannah Jones Lambert, died of childbirth complications. My father lost his mother, Margaret Brooks Elkins, when he was about five years of age from childbirth complications also.

My parents were married for 36 years until my father's death, August 31, 1959, from heart problems. My mother died many years later on May 22, 1988 from a stroke. We loved them and honor their memory.

My Parent's Marriage Certificate—1923

Mama Knew Best

Our mother, Alma Joy Elkins, was our salt of the earth and the main disciplinarian. She wasn't perfect, but a good person who taught us values, and hard work. Our father, as a law enforcement officer, had to work late into the night on Saturday and came home in the wee hours of Sunday morning. We never attended church on a regular basis, but Mama saw to it that we knew right from wrong. We were not even allowed to iron a blouse on Sunday. I remember saying "darn" one time and she practically washed my mouth out with soap. She thought that was a cuss word.

We were disciplined with the help of a little hickory switch (and probably deserved every lick) that immediately commanded our attention. It worked! I know this isn't politically correct. You would be charged with child abuse today or your child might sue you. That is how ridiculous things have become! She always made us do a chore immediately after the switching like "now go and fill up that wood box". I never quite figured that one out. Wasn't the whipping good enough? In her wisdom, I later realized she wanted us to think about the punishment and why it was necessary. By the time we went to the wood house and pouted a few minutes, everything was back to normal. She never said "this hurts me more than it hurts you" either! Mama always disliked anyone referring to young persons as "kids" rather than children. She would say "kids are something goats have!" She also said "no one would go unpunished for sins or wrongdoing." Her words of wisdom were "it will always come back to you."

She was always busy gardening, canning, cooking and trying to keep everyone on the right path. Mama was a fine seamstress, sewing for the home and making clothing for us.

My sister, Frances, was preparing to go to her graduation prom. The theme of the prom was a southern garden. Mama made Frances a long formal ball gown. The gown was made of pink chiffon with layers and layers of ruffles and lace. She even made roses for the dress and for Frances' hair by hand. Frances looked much like Scarlett O'Hara in *Gone With the Wind*. She was the "belle of the ball" that night.

Mama sacrificed much for her family and did without so we could have what we needed. Yet no one ever remembers hearing her complain. She often told us about her childhood days and how she walked a long distance to a one room schoolhouse even on snowy winter days. The school had one large stove in the center and several grades were taught in that one room by the same teacher.

To stay in touch with neighbors and abreast of happenings in the neighborhood, Mama talked with neighbors on the telephone. It became an important part of her life. We had a privately-owned party telephone line with glass insulators along the overhead telephone line. These insulators are now collected by antique enthusiasts. Since this was a party line where multiple families share the same phone line, each family had a particular ring pattern. Our family was assigned two rings. When we wanted to call someone, we cranked out the number of rings assigned to our neighbor. No push button phones on our farm! Later this line was torn down and replaced with public telephone service. We didn't have to crank the telephone any longer, but we had to call the operator and tell her the number we wanted. She dialed it for us. It is amazing the progress we have made in everything in so short a time.

Our family always ate in the dining room around a large table. Mama never allowed us to begin eating until our father came to the table. I guess she thought there would be nothing left after the children got through eating! These meals were cooked from scratch three times a day, a feat few attempt today. No microwave, frozen dinners or eating out!

Thank goodness Mama did have the help of Lulee with all these meals. Lulee lived on the farm and always helped with the washing and ironing and in any other capacity that was needed. When someone in Lulee's church died, Mama always made a funeral wreath for her. She cut a wreath frame from pasteboard and sewed lots of ferns and a variety of flowers on the pasteboard and tied it with a bow. What a lovely and thoughtful act (and art) of kindness. Lula Watson was a huge influence in the lives of my family. Her special story is told later.

Mama was a friendly, outgoing person and loved everyone. She even enjoyed meeting the mailman at the mailbox to just say hello and chat for a minute. Her life was mostly staying at home and raising seven children and that is saying quite a lot. We loved her very much and she left her mark for good in the world—especially our world!

In later years, Mama always had Pepsi Cola, mostly for the grandchildren.

My niece, Amber, was spending the night with Mama and it was bedtime. She began to beg for Pepsi Cola. She would say, "Grandma, I want some Pepi:" Mama would say, "It's too late for Pepsi." Amber continued to beg until my mother's patience was wearing thin. She had finally had enough after a few more pleads from Amber and said, "You ain't a gonna get no "Pepi"!

Every time the family is together, we tell the "Pepi" story and laugh just like we've never heard it before. We also repeat this when we say "no" about something today. It always brings laughter and a loving memory of our mother and her homespun, humorist expressions such as, "You ain't a gonna get no Pepi so just hush!"

Future generations need to know about their ancestry. It is important to have family members record these memories so future generations will know about their family roots. I am reminded of a special memory when I went back home to visit. I spent the night sleeping in the big room upstairs. Mama had fluffed up the thick feather bed and put fresh sheets on. The windows were raised and the cool night air came in along with the sound of frogs from the pond below. It was the same soothing sound I had heard so many times before as a child.

The next morning, I awakened to the fresh air blowing the thin, white curtains and the smell of bacon wafting into the room. Mama was up early, and as she had done so many times before, cooking breakfast for me. I experienced a flood of happy memories. I thought how the farmhouse and farm life as well as my mother's love shaped my life. All these experiences prepared me in many ways for future life experiences, good and bad. Lessons learned growing up on that farm help shape who I am and gave me the ability to accept life's challenges.

Another remembrance of our mother's love and care was shared by my brother Ted. He and his wife, Irene, came for a vacation one summer and Mama made fried apple pies. They really enjoyed them and the day they were going back home, she was up very early frying lots of chicken and making those fried apple pies. She wanted to make sure they had plenty to eat going home to Minnesota. Let's all hope our children remember us with that same loving kindness and giving attitude—most of all, unconditional love.

My daughter, Laurie, a talented poet in her own right, wrote a poem to honor her grandmother.

Grandma Elkins

When you have lived so long; then grow old
To young people stories and wise tales are told.
They tell us tales of their younger days
How hard it was in many ways.
They ask so little yet give so much
The glory of their love is just as such.
When the sad time comes for them to leave
In our hearts we'll see them again we must believe.
You are born; you live, and then you die
Please do not despair, do not cry.

We will all grow old and someday die
But never will you say goodbye.
We shall meet again in another place
It's so perfect; like Utopia, out in space.
Ones dear to us will always be a part
Tucked way down deep inside our heart.
Yes, Grandma is a woman who's grand
Tell her you love her and hold her hand.
Though she cannot hear
Her love and her soul is so near.
I do believe she is superior from all the rest
The older generation must be the best.

Laurie Lynn Cheek

Mama's Lovely Legacy of Flowers

As I work in my own garden today, I always think of my mom as she passed her love of gardening and growing beautiful flowers on to me. Mama managed to find time to have flowers blooming and bouquets in the house. She would gather Queen Anne's lace from the field. As I walk among the flowers in my garden, I enjoy the many old fashioned and now rare heirloom flowers my mother shared with me from her garden. It's as though she walks again with me and shares the beauty, especially when they are blooming in their glory. I feel her sweet presence once again long years after she has put down her shovel and hoe and passed this love of gardening to me. It is a legacy of beauty from one generation to another.

The family cactus blooms every Christmas without fail. This plant has been handed down for probably two hundred years. My Grandfather Lambert (Mama's father) attended a wedding and wore the original piece of the Christmas cactus in his lapel. He took it home and rooted it. Our cactus is from that same Christmas cactus plant. I continue to root cactuses now so I can hand them down to my children.

And so the love of gardening goes from one generation to the next. From great grandmother to mother, to daughter and hopefully, to grandchildren. I have passed many of the heirloom flowers from Mama's garden to my family and they in turn have shared them with friends and neighbors. Her flowers continue to delight and mean so much to so many.

Mama's legacy of gardening and the love of flowers still live in our family. Our daughter, Bonita, is teaching the names of the flowers to our young granddaughter, Ava. My sister, Frances, is an avid gardener and no doubt inherited Mama's special love of flowers. My sister, Margaret, has won numerous awards for her flower-arranging abilities. Margaret has passed this love and talent on to her granddaughter, Cameron.

Mama's garden lives on. She had many flowers which have now become heirloom flowers. I have made a list of some of those flowers which Mama shared with me.

Spirea—My favorite old fashioned spring flowering shrub from home. It blooms off and on all winter and then profusely in early spring.

Red Honeysuckle—This flower has blue-green foliage and scarlet flowers. It grew wild on the farm but is sold in garden centers everywhere today. Often this flower is grown as topiaries.

Daffodils—These old fashioned bulbs go back a hundred years. They are early bloomers and appear before most other bulbs.

Red Tulips—A type that blooms for many years without fail.

Tiger Lily—This flower is so beautiful and easy to grow. It has black speckled inverted petals with black seeds along the stalk which can be planted.

White Iris—This flower blooms in the very early spring long before others bloom.

Bridal Wreath Shrub—This is an old-fashioned spring favorite that blooms later in the spring season.

Feverfew—This reliable, medicinal herb has lovely white flowers resembling buttons. It is great for using in arrangements. All garden lovers should have this.

Dusty Miller—This particular very old variety has a different look not like any variety seen in garden centers.

Pink Dutsia—This early spring bloomer can be rooted easily.

Old Fashioned Running Rose—One of the oldest and most reliable varieties has a faint pink center and glossy foliage. This rose bloomed along our garden fence and what a show!

Yucca—This plant always blooms with stalks of creamy bell-shaped flowers during the summer.

Crepe Myrtle—This tree is a long-lived variety with lavender or pink blooms.

I have shared many of these heirloom flowers with other flower lovers who cannot find them in garden shops.

Mama's love of gardening is expressed in this favorite garden prayer.

The kiss of the sun
For pardon;
The song of the birds
For mirth;
One is nearer God's heart in a garden
Than anywhere else on earth!
Dorothy Frances Gurney

Some flowers or "pesky weeds" as they were called are now seen in gardening magazines and are very much in demand and grown in gardens everywhere. Some are very expensive and treasured. The maypop or passion flower is a very popular vine that grew wild on our farm. We enjoyed stepping on the green maypops just to hear the loud "pop." They are edible as they turn yellow when ripe. The juice from maypops is popular passion fruit.

Another weed was the reddish-orange trumpet vine that is sought after as a climbing vine which attracts hummingbirds. Hummingbirds are attracted to most trumpet-shaped flowers. This is sometimes called kite vine or hummingbird vine. The bright-orange butterfly weed is also popular. This plant attracts butterflies to your yard and is very showy. All of these grew in abundance on the farm. We spent many happy hours observing and enjoying these wildflowers as well as many more. We loved walking in the woods to find wild ginger with its attractive, mottled, dark green leaves. This plant was so very fragrant with the little 'pigs' seedpods underneath the leaves which also smelled of ginger. Many wild plants such as rat's vein with a beautiful, little white bloom grew under the pines. Very early spring sent us in search of pussy willow branches along the creek bank. We knew just the right spot to find every growing thing on the farm. That is where love of nature begins and remains always, enriching our lives and reminding us our world is such a beautiful gift.

Mama's Family—The Lamberts

Thomas Robert Lambert   Lula Hannah Jones Lambert

My grandfather, Thomas Robert Lambert, was born June 28, 1861 during the first year of the Civil War. His father, Robert P. Lambert, died in the Civil War when Thomas was only three years old.

My Grandfather Lambert married my grandmother, Lula Hannah Jones, April 2, 1889. Alma Joy Lambert Elkins, my mother, was the youngest in that family of three sisters including Rena and Bertha and one brother Oscar. My grandmother died at age 30 of childbirth complications when my mother was only 2 ½ years old.

The Civil War had devastating effects on both my mother's family as well as my father's family. Both our grandparents lost their fathers in the Civil War. The Civil War and post-Civil War years were tragic times for our families. They survived, however, and went forward with courage in spite of all the tragic setbacks and obstacles to live productive and honorable lives.

Daddy—Ruler of the Roost

My father, Tatum Thomas Elkins, played the violin, the banjo, and the piano by ear and sometimes sang. He was musically talented as well as an outgoing and friendly person. Often people would say they never saw him in town without a crowd of people around him.

As my dad was a law enforcement officer for twenty years, he had many tales to tell. Upon retirement, he was interviewed by the local paper and was asked what he planned to do. Daddy said he was going home, sit on the front porch in his rocking chair and after about three weeks would begin to rock just a little. As always, he planned and directed farm operations on a daily and detailed basis.

Daddy was a Navy veteran of World War I. He was the first person from Chatham County, North Carolina to enlist in the Navy after America entered the war. He sailed the Mediterranean and Adriatic Seas, as well as across the Atlantic Ocean four times. Dad served aboard the Leondas, a large coal burning anti-submarine and chaser-tender supply ship. It carried small anti-submarine boats and endeavored to bottle up German submarines in the Austrian and German submarine-bases along the Adriatic Sea coast between Italy and Greece. I remember a shell from Corfu,

Greece signed and dated. He served for two years and two days and was honorably discharged as a first class fireman.

While in the Navy, Dad had a small tattoo put on his wrist. He was always embarrassed by this so he wore a long-sleeved shirt to cover it. He said that was the "biggest fool thing he had ever done." If only he could see how much in style he would be today since they have become so popular among some!

After returning from the Navy, Dad became interested in politics and was voted Justice of the Peace. He was an auctioneer and did many auctions whenever time permitted. I loved listening to him demonstrate the colorful jargon of auctioneers just like the professionals. He must have been very good as people sometimes bid against themselves!

Dad must have loved his home in North Carolina. After his tour in the Navy, he stated that he had seen all the oceans and overseas lands he ever wanted to see and that he never expected to see them again. For the next forty-five years, I don't think he left the state of North Carolina or looked upon the waters of any ocean.

I recall times when Daddy would bring my sister Florence and me a brown bag of candy. He would put it under the front seat of the car on Saturday night. The first thing Sunday morning we ran out to see what kind of candy he had brought us. Daddy didn't generally express much affection openly so that bag of candy meant more to us than just the sweets. It was a way we knew he had remembered us.

Sometimes on Saturday or Sunday mornings when we were teenagers, my brother, my sisters and I would take Daddy's car and ride out in the country and have fun. We would turn on the siren as loud as possible. I don't think he ever knew what we did, as I think that was breaking the law!

We had a huge front yard with several two hundred year old tall, stately oak trees, so you can imagine the leaves we had to rake. My father insisted that we get every leaf when raking. We would say, "Tomorrow the ground will be full of leaves again!" He always said "Those won't! When you do something, do it right or not at all!" This taught us more than raking leaves. He was teaching us responsibility for what we do.

He was six feet in height and blessed with a strong body and sound mind for the majority of his life. Daddy was a highly self-sufficient person, believing, as he put it, "he could do about anything any other fool could do." My dad believed and practiced many of the philosophies of his father, often saying, "Anything that is worth doing is worth doing well."

Daddy believed in trying "to have something" stating that "any fool can make money, but it takes a smart man or woman to be able to save and accumulate for the future." This expression was used back then. He thought it unwise and foolish to make money with no thought of saving. He believed that anything you bought that you did not need always came with too high a price.

Like his father, he enjoyed music and could play most any kind of stringed instrument. His favorite was the fiddle or violin, which in the winter, he often played for relaxation after dinner by the fireplace or on the front porch in the summer.

While in the Navy, he went to a music store in Rome, Italy, to look for a violin. He was trying one out by play-ing a few American fiddle tunes when, within a very few minutes, a large group of delighted Italians had gathered. None could speak English, but they kept urging him to play for quite a long time. Apparently, they had never heard that sort of music played in those days. There were no records, CDs or Internet at that time so music from different cultures was a new experience. One can easily imagine the joy and spirit of that occasion.

He had a good sense of humor and enjoyed listening to and sharing a good story or joke. Most of the amusing stories were true ones about people he had known in the community over the years. He liked to tell of the time he shook the hand of President Franklin D. Roosevelt when he came through Pittsboro, North Carolina. Dad was helping to control the crowd as the Presidential car came to a halt where Dad was standing. President Roosevelt reached out and grasped his hand with a powerful handshake and said, "How are you, my friend?" "My friend" was a favorite term used by President Roosevelt. Dad recalled that he had the largest hands of any man he had ever seem—describing them almost as large as "small hams."

When my sister and I were in elementary school, we had to wait after school for about an hour for the bus to come. The school was nearby so we would go downtown, find our dad, and ask him for a dime for an ice cream cone from the drugstore. He always gave us the money. After buying the ice cream, we walked back to school to catch the long bus ride home. Each of us bought an ice cream cone as they were only a nickel apiece! Can you imagine?

I always thought Daddy had a lot of character, strength, and common sense. This was demonstrated when a neighbor, who apparently had a drinking problem, came by with beer and insisted my dad drink a beer with him. My dad invited him to sit on the porch and graciously took the beer and drank a little even though he really didn't drink. I thought there is my Dad, a sheriff, drinking a beer with this neighbor instead of putting him in jail! In those days, drinking was frowned upon and not accepted like social drinking is today. I was so mad and thoroughly humiliated. Later I realized he probably did a kind act and it was I who was insensitive and wrong.

As sheriff of Chatham County, he often said he never failed to arrest an offender once he went after them and never made an enemy as a result of the manner in which he handled an arrest. Often when he had an arrest warrant for someone, he would encourage that person to come in on his own thus saving the indignity of being arrested at home, perhaps before his wife and children. He never had to shoot anyone in doing his job, being a big, strong, no-nonsense person no doubt probably helped.

My dad was an honorable man and earned the respect of everyone for the manner in which he handled difficult situations with others allowing them as much human dignity as possible.

His respect for people paid off once, when he found himself in a difficult situation. A night raid on a moonshine still demonstrated this. He fell into a deep pit used to empty hot mash near the still. The fleeing man they were attempting to arrest immediately came back and pulled my Dad from the hot pit of mash and risked the possibility of going to prison as a result of being arrested. At the trial, the judge took into consideration the kind act and gave the man a suspended sentence. Doing the right thing and disregarding his own interests to help another paid off for him and my father. There must be a lesson there to put the needs of others before our own self-centered interests in order to make a difference.

A little known secret was that huge moonshine still operations were often financed by some upstanding citizens in the community and my dad was very aware of this. They were in the background and only people who worked the moonshine stills were ever caught and served time for illegal liquor operations. Some of these unnamed citizens profited greatly by supplying sugar, corn and whatever else was needed. Some became very financially secure while fronting these operations.

His concern for human dignity and courage was demonstrated when our beloved and respected family doctor struggled with alcohol. The doctor was on the street, not in the best form. My dad stopped and said, "Doc, get in this car" and put him in the car. He drove him to the Keely Institute Alcohol Rehabilitation Clinic in Greensboro, North Carolina. The time he spent there ended his struggle with alcohol and he was forever grateful to my father. He always felt he owed my dad a debt of gratitude and considered him his best friend for saving his life. My dad saw a person who needed some help and did something about it. I know it took character and courage to do that, after all, he was the town's doctor, loved and respected by all. The Keely Institute was originally Gov. Motley Morehead's home and today has been restored and preserved and is now known as Blandwood Mansion. It is a tourist attraction for Greensboro and used by many civic organizations and clubs.

My father told my brother Jim a story about when he was a young boy. During the long winter nights, he and his brothers would gather in the kitchen around the large stone fireplace. When they became hungry before bedtime, they would start slicing good country ham, which was always hanging in the pantry, and broil it over the fire. On one occasion their father shouted from the living room, "What are you boys doing back there?" They quietly replied, "Oh, nothing Pa! Nothing Pa! We're just doing a little cuttin' and frying, just a little cuttin' and frying!" He answered, "Yes, I bet you are, and I bet come next spring when all the ham is gone and you are eating sowbelly, you'll be doin' a little cussin' and crying!"

About six months before his twenty-first birthday, my dad approached his father about his first job. He said, "Pa, I am going to be twenty-one soon and I would like to get out and start making it on my own. Mr. Rufus Brewer has lined up a job on the railroad for me, and I would like to go ahead and accept it." His father immediately replied, "Boy, you can't be going anywhere, you're not twenty-one yet." In those days, on the farm, a young man was expected to work for his parents until age twenty-one. After some negotiating, his father, being a reasonable man, agreed to let him leave if he would hire someone to work in his place until his twenty-first birthday. My dad hired a local man, Gus Headen, and paid him fifty cents per day, with wages sent home from his railroad job for the next six months until he turned twenty-one. He respected his father, as well as the customs of the times and realized in those days that manpower was the lifeblood of a farm.

My father and his best friend, Walter Brewer, owned and operated a sawmill business in Chatham County. Walter was tragically killed at the sawmill as he became entangled in the log carriage and was pulled into the whirling saw, instantly killing him in a most horrible manner right before my fathers eyes. After that incident, Dad lost heart to continue the business. I'm sure this tragedy was hard to overcome, but he was able to move on and have a successful life. I think our negative experiences in life strengthens us and helps us to depend on that higher power so necessary for the spiritual strength that only comes from above. Otherwise, we try to carry everything on our own shoulders until the load becomes too heavy and we break down. We weren't designed by our Creator to live without His guidance. We only need recognize He is there to intervene and turn any circumstance into good and cover all things even bad, to work for our ultimate good. The word tells us, "The Lord Your God has great and wonderful things planned that you know not of." I believe that.

Seven years after my dad retired, he died suddenly August 31, 1959 of heart problems or a stroke at age 65. He was a Thirty-Second degree Mason and was buried with Masonic rites. He had a lot of character and shaped our lives for good. I loved my dad and miss him still.

Our Beloved Lulee

A very important person in our lives growing up was our beloved "Lulee" Watson. Her name was Lula, but we affectionately called her "Lulee." We loved her like a mother.

Soon after my parents were married, she often helped my mother and was there to assist when we were born. Birthing took place at home. Lulee was a midwife and helped with the birthing and rearing of all of us. Of course, our family doctor delivered each of us.

Lulee lived on our farm in the tenant house along with her husband, John, and two daughters. John had only one leg but a great deal of determination to be self-sufficient. He cut firewood by hand and dragged each limb with a rope. He took only a few steps at a time, using his good leg and a crutch to pull the heavy limb behind him. He split the wood by hand with an axe!

John made baskets of all kinds. He got the wood from a young, white willow tree from our woods and split the branches into thin strips to make large bushel baskets with handles. We used these to carry corn to feed the animals. He made other sizes and shapes as well. This was a very labor-intensive process of splitting, scraping and soaking the wood strips in water to make them flexible for the weaving process. He was willing to go through all this to create those beautiful handmade baskets. He sold the baskets for three to five dollars each. Imagine that! Today they would sell for hundreds. Many lessons in life can be learned from the lives of others that came before us.

John was quite a character when he was young. He lost part of his leg while trying to hop a moving train. He said this no doubt saved his life as he was so mean-spirited that he would surely have been killed by someone offended by his mean attitude and spirit. He preferred using a crutch and cane and could do almost any work. John was the child of slaves but went forward with courage and determination despite his handicap. John also liked to make home brew or wine from many things including rosebuds and dandelions. Quite a colorful character was he!

Mom told an amusing story about a time when John was pulling weeds in the garden. She heard John yelling loudly about mad hornets and throwing his arms around in the air. Mama ran out to see what the trouble was. John was looking around and yelling, "Laud Miss Alma! I'm in the middle of a mad hornet's nest! I can't see 'em but I sure can smell 'em!" Mama saw what was happening. She told John he was standing in the middle of her dill patch. That was what he was smelling. Mama got a real laugh that day. John had gotten fooled by a patch of dill. Hornets, when disturbed, give off a pungent dill-like odor as a reaction to stress.

With a life of hard work, Lulee asked for little and was thankful for what she had. Music was a large part of her life. She had an organ inherited from her mother and entertained us many times playing the organ, singing, and reciting poems she had written. She also played the piano, harmonica, guitar, and accordion—all by ear. She had no formal music lessons. Her musical ability was a gift.

Our "Lulee" had an unusual amount of self respect long before the civil rights movement. She just knew she was "somebody" and God's child. I vividly remember a time when she taught my sister and me a lesson in respecting everyone regardless of color or race. We were probably about five and eight years old, playing in our back yard singing a rhyme with the "N" word in it. About the same time, Lulee came around the house and looked at us with a frown and said "What did you say?" "I'm agonna tell your mammy on you right now!" I'll never forget it and we learned a valuable lesson that day. Just a scolding from Lulee was all it took. She had her own way of commanding respect.

Lulee often wrote songs and sang them to us. I do wish that I had been able to record these songs. I remember one about a tornado that swept through Greensboro in the 1940's. It went something like this:

God sent, God sent
A great tornado to Greensboro, North Carolina
God sent, God sent
A great tornado and it troubled everybody!
God moved, God moved
in Greensboro, North Carolina
on April, the second day
God moved in a great tornado
And many people were blown away.

That was the beginning. She sang these songs in a kind of chant. There were other verses, but unfortunately I can't remember them.

Another song or ditty, as she called them, Lulee liked to chant was
    White folks go to church in a big automobile
    Colored folks go to church straight through the woods and fields
    White folks go to church, they sit, talk, and smile
    Colored folks go to church and "Lord you can hear them half a mile!"
How true, how true! Gee's Grove, Lulee's church, was about two miles away and we could hear all that singing and clapping every Sunday! I only wish we had recorded her many songs and poems. We should preserve precious memories before they fade. I regret that I did not record my daddy playing his violin for my children.

Along with drinking lots of black Louisanne coffee, Lulee enjoyed dipping her snuff as the custom often was back then for many. Snuff is a mixture of different tobaccos. She always had a little dipping brush she made from a small stick. She chewed the end until it formed a brush to dip the snuff. Her round, silver snuff box was always tucked in her apron pocket. As children, we were fascinated with Lulee's snuff. My sister Flo and I mixed chocolate and sugar together and pretended we were dipping snuff just like

Lulee. We just pretended but never took up the real habit. Thank goodness! Mama saw to that!

Lulee came on Monday mornings to do the weekly wash. Water was heated to boiling in a huge black pot in the wash house. She boiled all the clothes in this huge pot and punched them down with a round stick. After boiling the clothes, they were transferred into a tin tub with a wash board. She scrubbed the clothes on the washboard with plenty of soap, rinsed them in another tub using bluing bleach to whiten the sheets and other white clothes. They were wrung out by hand and hung on the line outside with wooden clothes-

pins to dry. This ritual occurred each Monday. I can still see us running in and out of the fresh sheets drying in the warm sun and blowing in the wind. Children today probably don't realize how important clothes pins were back then to hang clothes on the line. No clothes dryers were available until much later.

Our clothes were ironed with black flat irons heated in front of the coals in the fireplace or on top of the stove in the kitchen, definitely a hot job during summertime. Later we would have electric irons.

Lulee helped us make butter about once a week The cream came to the top of the milk and was skimmed off and put into the churn. She hand churned it until it became butter and buttermilk with specks of butter left

in it. In my mind, I can still see her putting her hand down in that churn and bringing out gobs of golden butter. Salt was added to the butter and put into a butter mold to form and harden. We also ate the clabber, which is thick sour milk. The milk was allowed to sour and become solid looking something like cottage cheese. The cream was skimmed off to make butter. In later years, we had an electric churn to make butter.

A big event was sauerkraut making time. When the cabbage was ready to be picked, we gathered the large heads from the garden and removed the outer leaves. They were washed, cut up, and put into a large wooden barrel. The cabbage was layered with salt to make brine. Red pepper was added and all this was chopped until it was fine. Lulee helped chop the kraut. It was covered with cheesecloth and a round piece of wood. The wood was weighted down with a heavy white flint rock until the kraut was fermented and was later canned. There was a whole day of kraut canning going on! Little did we realize all that hard work making kraut would protect us from colds and flu viruses during the cold snowy winter. Studies have shown kraut may protect against Avian flu. A simple, healthful solution against a possible epidemic or pandemic that experts are so concerned about.

The most difficult chore Lulee had was making chitterlings. Chitterlings are the small intestines of pigs, which were cooked and eaten. It was a dirty job and was done in the wash house because its preparation smelled so bad. There was a huge black pot built into the fireplace with a chimney. This is where the chitterlings were cooked, the wash boiled, fat rendered for lard, and lye soap was made. After cleaning out the chitterlings, they were rinsed many times in large tin wash tubs and cooked in boiling water in the big black pot. Then the chitterlings were cooled, chopped up, rolled in flour and fried with vinegar and hot sauce. Lulee loved those "chittlins" and didn't seem to mind preparing them because she knew we always shared everything with her.

We loved Lulee as a family member and insisted that she eat at the table with us during a time when most black folks ate in the kitchen. Just to mention this makes me feel indignant but that's the way it was in the South back then. At least we have made

Lulee and my sister Florence

86

progress since then thanks to the civil rights movement. She was an important member of our family and treated with respect.

Neighbors often called on Lulee to help with all kinds of chores at which she was skilled such as being a midwife and aiding the sick. A midwife is a woman who assists women in childbirth. She also did washing and ironing for neighbors to earn extra money.

I'm most proud to say after Lulee retired at 100 years of age, she became famous in her own right as an entertainer. She provided entertainment for nursing homes and traveled all over the state to perform at daycare centers and for college students.

They paid her and explained about taking out for social security. She replied "that's O.K., I might need it when I retire." She was only 100 at that time!

She awoke each day and said, "Thank you Jesus", and fixed herself a strong cup of "100 proof Louisanne" as she called it. She loved strong black coffee so I don't think it will kill anyone. She would say, "Don't give me any coffee when I am able to see the spoon at the bottom of the cup." When asked what the secret of long life was, she quickly stated "black coffee and hard work!"

Often when Lulee sat in our kitchen sipping hot coffee we, as young children, would beg for some coffee. Knowing that Mama didn't want us drinking coffee, Lulee would support her by saying that coffee is what made her so black and she didn't think we wanted that to happen to us. That was the end of that! Lulee had a great sense of humor. She was so talented and actually a very intelligent soul with a world of experience and common sense about life. She was able to accept her lot in life with so much grace and dignity.

At one time, her little house caught on fire and almost burned down, but a neighbor put out the fire and saved it. I asked Lulee about the fire and wasn't she afraid. She replied, "No, because I knew where I would be either way." I think that was a powerful statement. As poor as she was here, she knew she had riches untold! I think that is the secret of her life in a nutshell. No wonder our family and many others loved her and saw something admirable about her.

Lulee died at the age of 104. On the last day of her life, she sang for the attending nurses in the hospital and probably drank some of that 100 proof black coffee too! Lulee's story was told in newspapers, featured in magazines like Reader's Digest, radio, television stations as well as CBS's Charles Kuralt's "On the Road." He said, "There is something noble and admirable about her." That was her legacy and her influence on our family as well as many others. Our beloved Lulee will live in our hearts always.

PART III

Descendents

Elkins Family Crest

Elkins

Family Descendents—From England to the Civil War

A poignant story from the Civil War provides a picture of our family roots and heritage. That time had devastating effects on our family. But links to our family heritage precede that era.

Our earliest recorded family heritage goes back to Anglo Saxon, Southern England along the Thames River Valley near London. The Normans of Viking and Scandinavian origin and the Germanic Anglo-Saxons gradually merged and spoke the English language.

John Elkins, a London merchant, was one of the incorporators of the London Company under which the first permanent colony was established in America at Jamestown, Virginia in 1607. William and George Elkins received Bachelor of Arts degrees from Oxford University on April 17, 1559. Ralph Elkins of Virginia is considered to be the progenitor of much of the Elkins family in the South. He came to Virginia around 1650 and died there in 1690.

His descendant, Stephen Benton Elkins, born September 26, 1841, had a remarkable life. He was admitted to the Missouri State Bar in 1864 and later moved to New Mexico and served as Territorial District Attorney, Attorney General, U.S. District Attorney and as United States Congressman for two terms. He moved to West Virginia and founded the town of Elkins in 1889. He had extensive investments in mining and railroads. He built a mansion in Elkins called Halliehurst. In 1891, he became Secretary of War and United States Senator from West Virginia in 1894. While serving as Senator, he and his father-in-law founded Elkins and Davis College located in Elkins, West Virginia. He sponsored the Elkins Railroad Act and the Mann-Elkins Act of 1910. His wife, Hallie Davis Elkins, is thought to be the only woman in America to have had a father, a husband and a son to serve as United States Senators.

Another descendant of Ralph Elkins was William Lukens Elkins. He became a large Pennsylvania oil producer and in 1875, joined forces with

John D. Rockefeller and Standard Oil Co. Later, he developed street railway projects in many states and his company controlled more trolley lines than any other company in America. He was a major benefactor to the city of Philadelphia supporting many worthwhile causes. The story of his life and accomplishments is contained in the book titled <u>Millionaires and Kings of Enterprise</u> by James Burnby, published in 1903. He died November 7, 1903 at age seventy-one.

Many other Elkins in early America achieved considerable success in their fields of endeavor. Henry W. Elkins (1847-1884) was a self-taught artist whose best known works are *Mount Shasta* and *The Thirty-Eighth Star*. William Lewis Elkins (1855—1933) was a noted American astronomer who became Director of Yale Observatory in 1896.

Our great grandfather was Joel A. Elkins born in 1809 in Chatham County, N.C. He married Sarah Harris to whom were born nine children, one of them James Franklin Elkins, my grandfather.

The Civil War began in 1861. This had tragic consequences for the Joel Elkins family. He was conscripted into military service in 1863 at the age of fifty-four. It was thought he was killed in action in Tennessee that same year. This must have been a desperate time in the South for a man of his age with nine children to be conscripted into military service. Even though he was a hatter by trade and made hats for the Civil War soldiers, he was still conscripted into the war. A story handed down through generations tells about a Confederate supply wagon train moving through Chatham County near Joel's home. Before daybreak on a Sunday morning, soldiers left his body in a pine box on the front porch of his home. Upon rising, his wife Sarah found his body. Imagine the horror of finding your deceased husband on the front porch knowing you were left with nine children for which to care. Those were the worst of times.

My grandfather, James Franklin Elkins, was only nine years old during that time. Two older brothers, Joseph and Oren, also served and survived the war. Joseph was captured near Richmond, Virginia in 1864 and released in April 1865. Oren was an artillery soldier and was with Robert E. Lee when he surrendered to Ulysses S.Grant at Appomattox, Virginia on April 9, 1865.

James Franklin Elkins, known as Jim, married Margaret Brooks while in his early thirties. They had five children. First born, Stroud Elkins died as a baby and James Shafter Elkins drowned at the age of twenty. My father, Tatum Thomas Elkins, was one of the surviving three children. Grandmother Margaret Brooks Elkins died of childbirth complications in 1888, when their youngest son, James Shafter, was about six months old. My grandfather was left with four children.

He later married his older brother's widow, Margaret Clark Elkins, in 1900 after his brother died in 1899 leaving seven surviving children in that family. Three of Margaret's ten children had died at that time. It was a custom, as in biblical times, that the death of a close relative meant the closest family member takes on the responsibility of the survivors. More than likely this was a blessing for both families although combined they totaled twelve children. Imagine dinnertime at the Elkins household!

James was age 46 and Margaret age 45 at the time of this marriage in 1900. All these children survived except James Shafter who drowned at the age of twenty in 1918. The irony of this was that he was known for his excellent swimming ability. He may have been too confident. He dove into a rain swollen river to go under and behind a torrent of water cascading over the dam. He never came up and his body was recovered the next morning downstream using a wire fence stretched across the swollen river. Our father and his brother, Durham, were overseas in the war at the time and did not get the news until months later. Shafter was almost twenty-one years old and was planning to go to war himself in a few weeks. He was an athletic young man and liked by everyone.

Shafter was a particularly unique individual. His most well known stunt was to ride two horses Roman style at a full gallop while standing up with one foot on the back of each horse as they ran side by side on his father's farm. It has been said that he was daring and fearless with a love of life. I wish I could have known him.

Shafter's death was another tragic time for my father's family. He was buried in the family cemetery along with his mother and oldest brother who died as a baby. Our Grandfather Elkins and Uncle Durham are also buried there. Their tombstones are the only ones visible today.

Our grandfather, James Franklin Elkins, was a prosperous cotton farmer who owned a drugstore, a blacksmith shop, and several rental houses in the Siler City, North Carolina area. He strived all of his life to have economic security for his family and rise above the insecurity his family experienced during those Civil War and post Civil War times. Remember, he was only nine years old when his father was killed in the Civil War leaving his mother with nine children to raise. Even so, with the tragic deaths my grandfather had to endure (the death of his wife and their first born son, and later an older son in a swimming accident) he persevered and rose above these personal tragedies.

The hardships of families living through the Civil War and the tragic consequences are hard to imagine leaving a legacy to attest to human perseverance and hard work. We can be proud that they left a legacy of lives of strength and courage.

As we encounter our own trials and tests such as the tragedy of September 11, 2001, may we reach out to others, love more and be strong for our families and future generations just as our ancestors are still an inspiration for us today.

My Grandfather, James Franklin Elkins

Elkins Family Photo (c.1908)

Taken at the two hundred-fifty acre farm in Siler City, NC. Standing, James Franklin Elkins, left on horseback, son Durham D. Elkins, second wife Margaret Clark Elkins, in the middle on the black horse was our father, Tatum Thomas Elkins at approximately fourteen years old at the time, and to the right on horseback, his younger brother, James Shaftner Elkins, who later in life tragically drowned before his twenty-first birthday. Beta Elkins, the oldest daughter had apparently already left home when this photo was taken.

Children Grow Up But the Farm Never Leaves Them

I have referred to my siblings throughout these reflections. There were seven children born of Tatum Thomas and Alma Joy Elkins, four girls and three boys. Eventually most of the seven moved to other areas and began their adult lives.

Margaret Elkins Vadersen is my beautiful oldest sister and she has my admiration for living life to the fullest after losing her husband, Bob Vadersen, after many great years of marriage. She, herself, fought and won a battle with cancer, demonstrating tremendous strength and courage. Margaret went to work in Norfolk, Virginia during World War II as a radio technician. There she met and married Bob Vadersen. He was in the family masonry business, but that was not his calling. He

later pursued construction sales and rentals, becoming a partner in Phillips Machinery Company located in Norfolk, Virginia. Margaret worked as a secretary for Virginia Medicare Systems until retirement. She has five children and seven grandchildren.

Jim Elkins served twenty six years in the U.S. Marines achieving the rank of Lt. Colonel. He was a war hero and won the Silver Star and Purple Heart for bravery during battle in Korea. His medic was killed and as leader of his platoon, he personally exposed himself to enemy fire to drag his men two at a time behind enemy lines to

administer first aid and save lives. He won a total of twenty-two medals for service in the Korean and Vietnam Wars. This exemplifies what courage is all about and what we are capable of doing.

While attending Elon College in Elon College, North Carolina, Jim played football, won track trophies, and graduated with honors. There he also met his lovely wife, Frances. They have five children and seven grandchildren. Frances has been a loyal supporter of Jim taking care of the children during his many military deployments. She retired after twenty-five years of teaching school!

Frances Elkins Langley is a very sweet person and has a lovely spirit. She is an avid gardener and grows beautiful flowers at their home in Pittsboro, N.C. She, like me, got her love of flowers and gardening from our mother. She and husband, Allen Langley, recently celebrated their fiftieth wedding anniversary. During their marriage, Frances and Allen owned and operated a motel and restaurant, called the Shady Rest, and a television repair and appliance store in Pittsboro, N.C. Allen also worked for a chemical manufacturing plant and served four years in the U.S. Air Force during the Korean War. They have four children and three grandchildren.

Ted Elkins has always had a love of the outdoors and observed nature and birds while on the family farm. He was the one who had a keen eye for finding arrowheads. He and his wife Irene live on a lake in Minnesota and grow beautiful flowers and a large vegetable garden. He enjoys fishing in the lakes and his hobby is carving ducks. Ted served in the United States Air Force for four years during the Korean War. For many years, he worked for a large trucking company located in the nearby St. Paul area and was a member of the Teamsters Labor Union. Irene is a native of Minnesota. Her grandparents came to this country from Sweden and  built the farm house in which she and Ted now reside. She has worked in retail sales and law enforcement. She has been a great supporter of Ted in married life, helping him recover from three heart attacks. They have one son Mark.

Jack Elkins followed in my father's footsteps and was the Chatham County Sheriff for many years. He lives with his wife Cora in a lovely home near the family home site in Siler City, North Carolina. They are retired and have a huge garden each year and flowers everywhere. Cora worked many

years as an office manager for a local manufacturing plant and is a valuable supporter of Jack in his personal and political life. Jack served two years during the Korean War as an United States Army paratrooper and was stationed at Fort Bragg, N.C. He was trained as an army medic and nearly lost his life on a jump when his parachute failed to open properly. He made it to the ground safely by hanging onto the top of another soldier's parachute.

When Jack was sheriff, our little town was much like the award-winning television series, "The Andy Griffith Show." In fact one of the characters from that series, Frances Bavier, who played "Aunt Bea," retired from television and settled in Siler City. This was very exciting for a small town. Jack and Cora have one daughter and two grandchildren.

I am next to the youngest in our large family. Flowers have always been an important part of my life going back to the family farm helping my mother plant and grow flowers. I was a floral designer and manager for many years and continue to garden and share flowers and plants with others. My husband, Wayne, was in regional electrical sales before retirement and enjoyed golf, flying and building model airplanes. He served in the

Mary and three of her children,
Eric, Laurie, and John

Korean conflict and was the personal driver for Colonel Scherrer. He also drove for General Bruce Clark, second in command in Korea and for Chief in Command General Maxwell Taylor. He was awarded the commendation medal for service there. Wayne has enjoyed painting landscapes as well as our "old home place", the Elkins family home. We live in Greensboro, North Carolina and have four children and four grandchildren. We love and enjoy our family and our precious grandchildren.

Florence (Flo) is the youngest in our family. She participated in many

school activities, was "Miss Siler City High", and a cheerleader. She worked for First Union Bank for many years. After retiring, Flo continues to work for the local newspaper and is married to Siler City Mayor Charles Turner. They enjoy three children and three grandchildren.

All of my family has the ability to adjust, face whatever necessary, and go forward with determination and resolve. This reflects, I think, those years on the family farm. Our life on the farm provided us with experiences and values. It strengthened our ability to face whatever we are confronted with in life with balance and integrity.

I am glad we survived our younger years and grew up on that farm together with the same father and mother. Bless them both! The benefits of that go on forever. I love you all.

Portrait of farmhouse—Painted by Mary's husband, Wayne.

Mary (third left) and sister Florence (fourth left) on a parade float celebrating the Fourth of July in Siler City.

PART IV

A Legacy of Flowers

Mama's Legacy Continues In My Own Garden

My love of nature and flowers in particular continue in all forms today sparked by my own mother's love of flowers. I credit her for any creative talents I have developed through the years all beginning on the family farm so long ago. The legacy goes on.

Beautiful heirloom flowers have been passed on to me from my mother's garden. One such flower is the early spring flowering shrub, Spirea. This shrub is beautiful for arrangements with other early spring favorites.

The Tiger Lily brings warm memories of my mother's garden.

This lily blooms each year without fail. Lovely!

Cleradendron is a lovely tropical vine with red and white flowers. This vine blooms all summer but is not hardy below 32 degrees.

This Red Honeysuckle Vine has scarlet flowers on bluish-green foliage. This running vine grew wild on the farm.

My interests and creativity extends from my garden and my flowers to carving wood flowers to making arrangements from nature's bounty. Some samples of my work are shared below.

Wood carved Lilies from my craft book —*A Forest Full of Flowers*

Woodland Violets: The violets are wood-shaved flowers and the leaves are green taffeta.

Other wood carved flowers from my book.

Creative Ideas To Share

Cactus Hat

Cactus Face

Halloween or Fall Scene

Grand Prize Winner

My Garden Party theme tablescape was the $600 Grand Prize Winner!

Japanese Garden

One of my greatest pleasures is my Japanese Garden that we have created in my backyard.

Appendix

This appendix contains additional poetry, an essay written by the author as well as pictures of the Cheek family.

Freedom and Liberty for All

We pay tribute and honor all those that have gone before and sacrificed so much. As a family and a nation we stand upon the principles for which so many gave their lives. We are not on this planet alone and have a responsibility to reach out and help others achieve their basic needs so necessary for preserving the peace and moral character of the world.

America was founded on Christian principles. Will we continue to honor these principles? We have our ancestors to thank for the life we enjoy today. The sacrifices they made ensure that we will have justice and liberty for all. We must honor their sacrifices or cease to enjoy freedom and justice for ourselves and our posterity. Our faith, families, and freedoms are most important. I am proud that our nation is reaching out to defend other nations who are in bondage and helping to secure their basic human liberties. It is not enough to continue to enjoy our way of life while turning a blind eye to others who live under tyranny and torture.

I am proud to be an American with the privileges we enjoy. May God continue to bless our great nation as we reach out to help others. Only then will our own security ultimately be assured. I believe in justice, peace, hope and equality for all. We are still together on planet earth, one world under God. Our most noble purpose in life should be justice for all. Someday we will be able to say "E Pluribus Unum" (out of many one) for the whole world!

Each person is of infinite value because we are created in the image of God.

AMERICA
PREFERENCE OR PRINCIPLE

Author's Note:
This poem is dedicated to our forefathers and the principles for which they lived and died.

Our nation was founded on God's principles
Now we invite disaster with our godless preferences.

We must not violate what made us so great
All can still choose Gods way before it's too late.

The Lord gives liberty and freedom to all
Honor Him first or our nation will fall.

And the fall will be felt with ever increasing division and strife
The enemy will come and take over our way of life.

If His hand of protection is taken from our land
Against the enemy we'll never be able to stand.

We violate His principles by what we do
And pass laws directed against God imposed by only a few.

We either stand and fight for our freedoms before it's too late
Or see our nation fall and the fall will be great.

It's not about you or I or about our wants
It's about honoring God and following His ways.

Pray for our leaders to honor the principles of God
And the paths our forefathers have trod.

God will honor our nation if we repent and pray
It's time to turn our land back to Him without delay.

We must recognize our peril and plight
Or we'll cease to see His protection and light.

Oh! Give us the courage and boldness to do
What it takes to turn America back to you.

Our nation is being weighed in the balance
The scales will tip for terror if we continue this silence.

We practice immorality and want it legalized
This is setting ourselves up to be terrorized.

We have taken prayer and the bible out of our schools
The Ten Commandments and Christian symbols are ridiculed.

Some want God out and personal preference in
How long can we survive if our people allow only a few to win?

Everyone must fight for our freedoms today
Pastors and Christians please stand in the gap for our nation and lead the way.

Stand up with conviction for the truth we know
Then God will protect and bless our nation from all our foes.

Cry out to God for mercy and grace
He will surely bless and turn us back to see His face.

Oh! Lord, bless us once again we pray
Don't let a few determine our fate today.

Mary Elkins Cheek
October, 2004

Mary Elkins Cheek in her early twenties

Afterword

Happiness

We search for happiness
in all the wrong places.
Happiness can never be found
in riches and fame, treasures or pleasures.

Small kindnesses to brighten
lives around you today
May contain the seeds of salvation
for someone along the way.

A long life we may live
Will surely be measured
by the love and happiness we give.

Just share that love with others
And you will see
The love you give flows back
in blessings so free.

Mary Elkins Cheek

About the Author

Mary Cheek's life-long passion for gardening and flowers began on the family
farm observing and helping her mother
plant and grow flowers. She continued
her interest in flowers and spent many
years as a member and Past President
of her garden club; learning, exhibiting
flowers, and was a blue ribbon winner in
flower shows.

Her interest and experience with
flowers later led to a profession. She was
a floral manager for many years before
retirement. Now she spends time in her
own Japanese Garden as an interesting project; a peaceful, spiritual place
of retreat in our fast-paced world. Mary recommends staying close to the
land, growing and sharing plants. She describes her gardening experience
as therapeutic and a wonderful way to relax.

This is Mary's second book. Her first, titled "A Forest Full of Flowers"
was a craft book on wood-shaved flowers. She taught many classes and was
featured on television, in newspapers, and magazine articles. She freelanced
an article about her flowers in *Early American Magazine*.

In "Where Whippoorwills Sing" she lists and describes many heirloom
flowers and others that grew on the farm and now grow in her own yard.

From **Mary's Book on Flowers**—
Never hurry and don't worry
We're here for just a short visit
So don't forget to stop and smell the flowers!

Cheek Family Photos

Our Grandchildren

978-0-595-43839-6
0-595-43839-3